Speaking in Parables

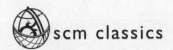

scm classics

Speaking in Parables

A Study in Metaphor and Theology

Sallie McFague

scm press

© Sallie McFague 1975
Preface © Gerard Loughlin 2002

A catalogue record for this book is available
from the British Library

ISBN 0 334 02874 4

First published in Britain in 1975 by SCM Press
This new edition published in 2002 by SCM Press
9–17 St Albans Place, London N1 0NX

www.scm-canterburypress.co.uk

SCM Press is a division of
SCM-Canterbury Press Ltd

Typeset by Rowland Phototypesetting Ltd,
Bury St Edmunds, Suffolk
Printed by Nørhaven Paperback A/S, Viborg, Denmark

To Gene

Contents

PART II

Preface

The academic practice of theology can, at times, seem overly concerned with abstruse and subtle arguments about method and procedure, with conceptual clarification and interpretative licence, with almost anything except what matters most. No doubt theology has to be like this, because it is charged with thinking the Church's faith in all possible dimensions. Theology has to go all the way with believing that the world is bestowed rather than accidental, a gift rather than happenstance, and this requires engaging with all the myriad ways of the world. Thinking faith through to the end is an endless task, since human thought is both ever changing and frustratingly complex and the world has a stupefying capacity for surprise and perturbation. And yet, when all is said and done, theology is concerned with that most universal of human interests (after eating, sleeping and copulating), namely the telling of stories.

Theology can seem at its driest and most arcane when it is concerned with the minutiae of biblical exegesis and worrying about the Bible's historical veracity and contemporary relevance. And yet it is then that theology is concerned with the stories by which it seeks to live, which are themselves about a man who told stories, whose own life story became the context in which the Church continues to narrate the very tale by which it is constituted. The *priority* of the story – the story of Jesus variously narrated and typologically augmented in earlier and later tales of Hebraic heroes and Christian saints – is now well established by the 'narrative theology' that came to prominence in the late 1970s and early 80s. It was and is a theology that seeks to return to the story-telling matrix of the Christian faith in order to remember that, no matter how clever and necessary the speculations of theologians, what finally matters are the scriptural and ecclesial stories by which lives are shaped for glory. Theology is ordered towards preaching, not so much as pulpit proclamation but as lived narration, the witness of enacted stories and Christ-formed lives. As Sallie McFague puts it in *Speaking in Parables*, 'the task of theology is to serve the hearing of God's word, that strange truth that disrupts our ordinary world and moves us – and it – to a new place' (p. 32).

How theology can move us to a new place is the concern of Sallie McFague's *Speaking in Parables: A Study in Metaphor and Theology*. When it was published in 1975, this was one of the first and most sprightly works of 'narrative theology'. Other, heavier, names are perhaps now more readily associated with this kind of theology, but McFague was one of its pioneers, profoundly aware that a theology of movement requires the transport of imagination. As the titles of McFague's next two books indicate – *Metaphorical Theology: Models of God in Religious Language* (1982) and *Models of God: Theology for an Ecological, Nuclear Age* (1987) – her interests were wider than a narrow 'narrative' framework and have increasingly focused on ecological concerns, as the titles of her more recent books show: *The Body of God: An Ecological Theology* (1993) and *Super, Natural Christians: How We Should Love Nature* (1997).

To some extent, McFague has distanced herself from her first book, which is more obviously 'orthodox' than her later writings, where she has developed a pantheistic account of the God–Nature that human beings inhabit. In the earlier book there is a keener sense of the transcendent God who confronts us in and through the stories told by and about Jesus, the Word in the words of human imagination. While distancing herself from both Karl Barth and Rudolf Bultmann, she maintains a Barthian sense of God's 'otherness' as mediated through the scriptural witness, and a Bultmannian stress on the challenge that this witness poses to those who hear its call. Theological reflection is about keeping 'Christian language, believing, and life close to its primary model, the parable, so that, like the parable, it helps people to be encountered by the word of God' (p. 75).

While some of McFague's later interests are already evident in *Speaking in Parables*, especially a concern with the natural, bodily nature of spiritual life, the book is primarily concerned with the parabolic character of Christian proclamation, the metaphorical content of Christian story-telling. McFague argues that metaphorical movement is at the heart of human thought and creativity; it enables us to inhabit and be inhabited by the world and to make it new.

Metaphor is, for human beings, what instinctual groping is for
the rest of the universe – the power of getting from here to
there. . . .We do this through a process in which the imagination
is the chief mover, setting the familiar in an unfamiliar context
so that new possibilities can be glimpsed. (p. 46)

At one level, metaphor is merely a trope, a figure of speech by which
we speak about one thing in terms of another. The metaphor thus
transports a range of resonance and allusion from one term to
another, so that the writhing of the snake, with all its connotations,
becomes that of the script. One result of such rhetorical analysis is
an awareness of the use of metaphors in scriptural and religious
discourse, for example regarding the fatherhood of God. That we
call God *abba*, and might call her mother, affects how we think and
feel about God and about our own parents. But from considering
discrete metaphors we can move to considering language as itself a
metaphorical process in which there is no point where terms are
stable and irredeemably fixed to certain objects. All terms move,
and those that appear fixed and stable have merely become so slow
that we think they are dead metaphors. So now, for example, when
we 'conceive' an idea, we don't think of it as a result of having sex.

McFague is particularly interested in the open-ended and ambiguous effects of metaphorical displacement, because it is never fully possible to predict or control the range and resonance of meanings that result
from seeing one thing in terms of another. Metaphor affects not only
how we *see* the world, as we say, but also how we *feel* about things, the
way in which we inhabit the world. This is not least because so many
metaphors are bodily and thus a means by which we extend our body
into the world and connect it with other bodies. Indeed, for McFague,
following Elizabeth Sewell, metaphor is a means of connection or
copulation, an erotic movement by which we embrace the world. 'The
unknown lies all about us and we "figure" it all with ourselves – the
human metaphors. Our movement, of whatever sort, is always metaphorical, with ourselves as one term of the metaphor' (p. 48).

Needless to say, the foregoing arguments depend upon a series
of metaphorical moves that illustrate the priority of the metaphorical;
it is never secondary to, or an embellishment of, some prior and
pristine use of language that somehow escapes the instability, the
desire for movement, of language itself. Thus McFague's theology is

resolutely set against those positivist philosophies and theologies that assume that the world can be named in some objective and perspicuous manner, unclouded by the shiftiness of language. Instead, she celebrates the way in which, as if of itself, language is able and wants to take us to new places and show us how the world might appear differently as we move and are moved by our words. For this is how parables work; they are, as McFague argues, extended metaphors, stories that, like metaphors, take us somewhere else. Moreover, we can never be certain where they are taking us. Parables are not didactic, simple allegories with coded messages that we can simply read off after reducing the story to an injunction or moral prescription. Instead of interpreting the parable, we must enter its world and risk finding ourselves interpreted, translated into a new context, a world in which the first are last, those we passed in the street guests at the table, and the newcomer rewarded equally with us who have laboured all day.

The metaphoricity of the parable is its power to so move us that the world appears to us newly, that we see it as if for the first time. This dynamic of the metaphor extends not only to the parables of Jesus, but also to the Church's parables about Jesus and to Jesus himself, who is the prime metaphor, the transport of the Christian movement. 'A parable of Jesus is not only an interesting story; it is a call to decision issued from one who in some way or other is himself a parable, or, as Christians believe, *the* parable of God' (p. 65). In McFague's parabolic theology, 'metaphor' and 'parable' themselves become metaphors for what Jesus effects in the world in the story that he is and becomes, a story that has the power to move and connect, to metaphorize the world into the Kingdom of God. Thus Jesus is the true metaphor, the word that moves.

Gerard Loughlin
Senior Lecturer in Religious Studies
University of Newcastle upon Tyne
Advent 2001

Introduction

The purpose of theology is to make it possible for the gospel to be heard in our time. That is a formidable task. To many of us it seems an impossible task. In a post-Christian, secularized culture, theologians had barely recovered their breath after the 'death-of-God' era when they were plunged into the radical subjectivity and drug-induced raptures of the counter culture, followed by a brief respite in the theology of play and the now current political theology. But the purpose of theology remains untouched: men and women who do theology are under the same command they always have been under, that is, to help the word of God be heard. Some say that God's word needs no help – it can do its own work where and when it will – and finally, of course, that is true, for the mysteries of faith are beyond human control. But no theologian pretends to that work anyway; the most he or she would claim to be is a clearer of fields, a preparer of the soil. And it is this job – the job of making the gospel credible or possible – that seems so difficult to us nowadays.

But risks must be taken, for safe theology today is no theology at all. We live in a time of personal and social confusion and skepticism, a time that, for all its newly emerging religiosity, is a secularized and disbelieving time. If a person is a Christian and by vocation a theologian, then the task at hand is to help this society hear the good news. The assumption of the present book is that theology could better fulfill this function were it to attend to Jesus' parables as models of theological reflection, for the parables keep 'in solution' the language, belief, and life we are called to, and hence they address people totally. If theology becomes overly abstract, conceptual, and systematic, it separates thought and life, belief and practice, words and their embodiment, making it more difficult if not impossible for us to believe in our hearts what we confess with our lips. There is a way to do theology, a way that runs from the gospels and Paul through Augustine and Luther to Teilhard and the Berrigans, that one could call intermediary or parabolic theology, theology which relies on various literary forms – parables, stories, poems, confessions – as a way from religious experience to systematic theology.*

The credibility gap between thought and life, theology and personal existence, the gospel and contemporary society, is one which, given the nature of the form in which we have the good news, never should have occurred. For the parables of the New Testament, the passion story, and Paul's writings are not ideas to which a spectator must somehow relate him- or herself, but stories of men and women whose lives are one with their thought. If one sees such genres as sources of theology, then whatever else theology may be, it is not 'incredible,' not something apart from my life, your life, or the life of our contemporary society. It is fearfully personal, which is to say, of course, fearfully social as well, for stories are always about persons in relation to their world. And being personal in this way means also that theology is radically concrete, for there is no such thing as 'a person in general,' as the parables, and the confessions of Paul and Augustine, so painfully and gloriously illustrate.

The parable is a prime genre of Scripture and certainly the central form of Jesus' teaching. Current scholarship sees the parable as an extended metaphor, that is, as a story of ordinary people and events which is the context for envisaging and understanding the strange and the extraordinary.† In the parabolic tradition people are not

---

* Such theology is truly an interdisciplinary venture and many contemporary American theologians are currently involved in it. I find the work of the following theologians particularly helpful: David Burrell, Stephen Crites, John S. Dunne, Ray L. Hart, William F. Lynch, H. Richard Niebuhr, and Richard R. Niebuhr. All of us are, in one way or another, interested in the role of the imagination in theological reflection and we find ourselves dependent on the writings of various Biblical scholars on parable (Robert W. Funk, Dan O. Via, Amos N. Wilder) and of philosophers and literary critics on story, poetry, and metaphor (Erich Auerbach, Owen Barfield, Max Black, Martin Heidegger, Susanne Langer, Elizabeth Sewell, Philip Wheelwright).

† Much interesting work to which I am indebted is currently being done on parables as metaphors; see, for instance, Amos N. Wilder, *The Language of the Gospel: Early Christian Rhetoric* (New York: Harper and Row, 1964), re-issued as *Early Christian Rhetoric: The Language of Gospel* (Cambridge: Harvard University Press, 1971); Robert W. Funk, *Language, Hermeneutic, and Word of God: The Problem of Language in the New Testament and Contemporary Theology* (New York: Harper and Row, 1966); Dan O. Via, Jr., *The Parables: Their Literary and Existential Dimension* (Philadelphia: Fortress Press, 1967).

asked to be 'religious' or taken out of this world; rather, the transcendent comes *to* ordinary reality and disrupts it. The parable sees 'religious' matters in 'secular' terms. Another way to put this is to speak of Jesus as the parable of God: here we see the distinctive way the transcendent touches the worldly – only in and through and under ordinary life.

If Jesus as the parable of God, as well as Jesus' parables, are taken as models of theological reflection, we have a form that insists on uniting language, belief, and life – the words in which we confess our faith, the process of coming to faith, and the life lived out of that faith. And at each of these levels we discover the necessarily parabolic or metaphoric character of our confession, for Christian language must always be ordinary, contemporary, and imagistic (as it is in the parables); Christian belief must always be a process of coming to belief – like a story – through the ordinary details of historical life (as it is in the parables, though in a highly compressed way); Christian life must always be the bold attempt to put the words and belief into practice (as one is called to do in the parables).

A theology that takes its cues from the parables finds that the genres most closely associated with it are the poem, the novel, and the autobiography, since these genres manifest the ways metaphor operates in language, belief, and life. Hence they are prime resources for a theologian who is attempting an intermediary or parabolic theology – a theology that is, on the one hand, not itself parable and, on the other hand, not systematic theology, but a kind of theology which attempts to stay close to the parables.* Such theology may not be the major tradition in Christian theology, but nevertheless it is an important tradition, as evidenced, for instance, by Paul's letters, Augustine's *Confessions*, John Woolman's *Journal*, Kierkegaard's writings, Bonhoeffer's *Letters and Papers from Prison*, or Teilhard's theological writings. The hope is that such theology will surface as a major genre, for it attempts to serve the hearing of God's word for our time by keeping language, belief, and life together in solution.

---

* I am indebted to Michael Novak, in a letter dated October 25, 1971, for the idea of what I call intermediary theology. 'In between imaginative literature and academic theology there is a form of intelligence which is precise, discursive, and analytical, but also in touch with concrete experience and with the imagination. *That* is the model for academic intelligence.'

As has been said, parables are metaphors. Parables are stories, of course, but of a particular kind – stories that set the familiar in an unfamiliar context, which is also what a metaphor does. A metaphor is a word used in an unfamiliar context to give us a new insight; a good metaphor moves us to see our ordinary world in an extraordinary way.

> In Florida consider the flamingo
> Its color passion but its neck a question.
> > (Robert Penn Warren)
> > my salad days
> When I was green in judgment.
> > (Shakespeare)

What is at issue, of course, is not just metaphor as a useful (or even a necessary) means of communicating something we already know. This would be allegory, not metaphor. Rather metaphor is a way of *knowing*, not just a way of communicating. In metaphor knowledge and its expression are one and the same; there is no way *around* the metaphor, it is not expendable. One can insist that certain metaphors are incorrect or inappropriate or do not 'fit,' but then all one can do is suggest other metaphors that are preferable. One cannot do without *any* metaphors.

To say, for instance, that Jesus is 'the Messiah' or 'the Logos' does not mean that these are useful images which will convey to the populace what the *cognoscenti* (those who are in on the real truth behind the images) have in some purer form. The insight or revelation comes *with* the metaphor – they are given together. As in poetic inspiration, the knowledge and its expression come together in a flash – poets, for instance, cannot 'say' what they want to say apart from metaphors. Presumably they have an intimation, inchoate and confused, of something new that they are attempting to bring to the surface and express, but the only way of grasping it, of pointing to it, is through the recognition of certain ordinary words as the 'right' ones to serve as the 'grid' or screen – a way of seeing – for what is not perceivable directly.* Likewise, to suggest that

---

* For expansion of this notion of metaphor as grid or screen, see Max Black's essay, 'Metaphor,' in *Models and Metaphors: Studies in Language and Philosophy* (Ithaca: Cornell University Press, 1962), pp. 24–47.

Jesus is the Messiah says something about Jesus in terms of all the Hebrew paraphernalia of messiahship. It is a grid which highlights certain things and depresses others, and this *is* our knowledge of Jesus (this image and many others – servant, brother, Logos, healer, shepherd, king, and so on).

To say, then, that a New Testament parable is an extended metaphor means not that the parable 'has a point' or teaches a lesson, but that it is itself what it is talking about (there is no way *around* the metaphor to what is 'really' being said). Thus to say that the parable of the Prodigal Son is a metaphor of God's love suggests that the story has meaning beyond the story of a human father and his wayward son, but that only through the details, the parable itself, are we brought to an awareness of God's love that has the shock of revelation. If the story of the Prodigal Son tells us about that love, it does so indirectly, for the story *itself* absorbs our interest. We do not, I think, naturally allegorize it (is the father 'God'? is the feast a symbol of 'the kingdom'?). The story is 'thick,' not transparent; like a painting, it is looked *at*, not through. William Wimsatt, the literary critic, says that a stone sculpture of a human head refers to a particular human head, to be sure, but what interests us – and what may ultimately illumine our appreciation of that 'real' head – is concentration on the *carved* head before us. The story of the Prodigal Son is a sculpture, a metaphor, of something we do not know much about – human becoming and God's extraordinary response.

The world of the parable, then, includes, it *is*, both dimensions – the secular and the religious, our world and God's love. It is not that the parable points to the unfamiliar but that it includes the unfamiliar within its boundaries. The unfamiliar (the kingdom of God) is the context, the interpretative framework, for understanding life in this world. We are not taken out of this world when we enter the world of the parable, but we find ourselves in a world that is itself two-dimensional, a world in which the 'religious' dimension comes to the 'secular' and re-forms it.

There are other kinds of worlds; for instance, there is, in mystical traditions, the possibility of a 'religious world' where we are encouraged to leave behind all that is secular, temporal, human, political, fleshly. And there is a flat, 'secular world' which is nothing other than human and historical; such a world has no other dimension that informs it. But the parabolic world is neither of these – it is neither secular *nor* religious but both at once. And the implication is that there is no true human life that is either secular *or* religious. Dante knew this in the *Divine Comedy*, for he envisioned paradise as a world in which *all* that is human is taken up and transformed, a world in which nothing human is lost. Teilhard knew this also in his grand evolutionary march of the natural and the human towards its fulfillment. Such visions are on a continuum with the world of the parable because they say that the world, the true world, is *at one and the same time* two-dimensional. We do not live in a secular world that must be discarded when we become 'religious,' nor do we live in a 'religious' world which has no truck with the secular; the parabolic world shows us another possibility (and this is what the incarnation is about) – that 'God is with us' in, through, under, and for our human, historical, temporal world. In such a perspective, the doctrines of creation and redemption take on a new meaning – *God himself* formed the world and re-forms it, the world was never without his power and presence, it was never alone. Nor will we ever leave it behind – faith in the resurrection of the *body* is the shocking assertion that true life is forever two-dimensional, the assertion that the world of the parables is *the* world, known now only in prolepsis and in secret, but on a continuum with that time when the city of the world and the city of God shall be one.

A theology that is informed by parables is necessarily a risky and open-ended kind of reflection. It recognizes not only the inconclusiveness of all conceptualization when dealing with matters between God and human beings (an insight as old as religion itself), but also the pain and skepticism – the dis-ease – of such reflection. Theology of this sort is not neat and comfortable; but neither is the life with and under God of which it attempts to speak. The parables accept the complexity and ambiguity of life as lived here in this world and insist that it is in *this* world that God makes his gracious presence known. A theology informed by the parables can do no less – and no more.

Like all theology, however, its purpose is to be a servant of the hearing of God's word in a particular time and place. Theology is, then, always hermeneutical, always concerned with how the gospel can be 'translated' or understood – grasped – by people. This is not, of course, merely a problem of renewing biblical images now grown into clichés or of communicating information, but the more basic problem of serving the hearing – and acceptance – of the word of God. Such hearing and acceptance in the parables takes place through imaginative participation when an old word or story or event is suddenly seen in a new setting, an insight with implications for one's belief and life. We will necessarily be concerned, then, with how insight occurs through language, how one comes to this moment of belief, and how one works it out in all of one's life. Coming to belief through insight and the life that then ensues – this parabolic model – has deep implications for theology: it is these implications which form the heart of the present essay.

The plan of my modest attempt in this book falls into two main parts, a foundational part and a constructive part. The foundational chapters will look at metaphor and parable as basic forms which provide for theological reflection a method of uniting life and thought. Preceding these basic formulations will be a chapter attempting to give an overview through concrete examples of where we are headed and another chapter reflecting on some crucial problems in contemporary theology to which intermediary or parabolic theology speaks. The second part will deal with some forms of Christian reflection – the poem, the story, and the autobiography – as sources for parabolic theology as it attempts to integrate language, belief, and life. This essay is, for me, merely 'on the way', it does not present an example of the kind of theology it calls for.* The present work suggests a method and resources toward such a theology; another book of another sort is called for eventually, because if metaphor is the method, the result will be more like a parable than a system. The reader should know that an overview of the argument of the book has appeared in my article entitled 'Parable, Metaphor, and Theology' in the December, 1974 issue of the *Journal of the American Academy of Religion*.

My debts are many. I feel my efforts in this book are a small contribution to the work of an emerging company of American theologians who increasingly see the importance of story and parable

---

* Two books which, in different ways, are examples of the sort of theology I have in mind are Richard R. Niebuhr, *Experiential Religion* (New York: Harper and Row, 1972) and William F. Lynch, *Images of Faith: An Exploration of the Ironic Imagination* (Notre Dame: University of Notre Dame Press, 1973).

for Christian reflection. My own work has for a number of years been deeply influenced by that of Erich Auerbach, Robert Funk, William F. Lynch, H. Richard Niebuhr, and Amos Wilder. I am especially indebted to a few people who have read and offered criticisms of this work: Mara Donaldson, Mary Lee Kelly, Michael Novak, Sr. M. Aquin O'Neill, Timothy Sedgwick, and George Stroup. Finally, I have been supported in innumerable ways by Eugene TeSelle who, in the mundane and often trying demands of family and professional existence, has lived out his belief in the equality and liberation of women. To him this book is dedicated in gratitude.

Part I

I

A Trial Run:
Parable, Poem,
and Autobiographical Story

A trial run is a worthwhile enterprise. Many books use the first five chapters to give historical background, then refute other views, and only in the final chapter (usually called 'Prolegomena to Some Theological Directions') is there a clue given to what the author has been up to. I would rather attempt a trial run, which, full of holes and unsubstantiated assertions, nevertheless gives the reader some clue as to how the theory might shake down in practice. In this brief chapter we will do no more than look in some detail at a few examples of literary genres that have been used for religious reflection. The stress in this chapter, more than in the rest of the essay, is on detail, for the crucial point here is to persuade the reader with a few well-known examples from Christian letters that parabolic theology is not a theory to be *applied to* literary genres of the Christian tradition but a kind of reflection that arises *from* them. Such persuasion will be effective only if the details of a parable or a poem can be shown to substantiate, even to demand, such an approach.

Theological discourse, and especially 'God-talk,' during what has been called the 'absence' or the 'death' of God, is, as we all know, in trouble. Richard Rubenstein, the Jewish theologian, states the problem this way:

> Contemporary theology reveals less about God than it does about the kind of men we are. . . . Today's theologian, be he Jewish or Christian, has more in common with the poet and the creative artist than with the metaphysician and physical scientist. He communicates a very private subjectivity.[1]

And Sam Keen says that

> for the moment, at least, we must put all orthodox stories in
> brackets and suspend whatever remains of our belief-ful attitude.
> Our starting point must be individual biography and history. If
> I am to discover the holy, it must be in *my* biography and not
> in the history of Israel. If there is a principle which gives unity
> and meaning to history, it must be something I touch, feel, and
> experience.[2]

Several similar chords are struck in these two statements: the
insistence that theology be existential, personal, sensuous; the wari-
ness with which both Rubenstein and Keen approach talk *about*
God; an intimation that a way out of the dilemma may be through the
language and methods of the poet and storyteller. Their insistence on
existential, sensuous, religious reflection that tells stories about
human life and only by implication speaks of God is not as radical
as it might at first blush seem, for it is an old and vibrant tradition
in Western Christendom. We see it everywhere in the Old and New
Testaments – in the history of Israel in its covenant with God and
the many little stories that reflect that big one (Abraham and Isaac,
the exodus from Egypt, Saul and David, and so on) and in the story
of Jesus of Nazareth, which again is the central story reflected in many
little stories, principally the parables. Worldly stories about human
beings in their full personal, historical, bodily reality is also the 'way'
of Augustine's *Confessions*, of Dante's *Divine Comedy*, of John Donne's
religious sonnets, of John Bunyan's *Pilgrim's Progress*, of Milton's
Paradise Lost, of John Woolman's *Journal*, of George Herbert's sacramental poetry, of Kierkegaard's work as an author, of T. S. Eliot's
'Wasteland,' of Teilhard de Chardin's letters and writings from the
trenches. There are many indications that the *kind* of theological
discourse Rubenstein and Keen are groping for is not only appropriate to the Judaic-Christian heritage, but is *called for* by it.

In order to get a few more solid clues to the nature of such
discourse, let us look at three examples of religious reflection all
concerned with God-talk, a parable, a poem, and an autobiographical
story: the parable of the Prodigal Son, Gerard Manley Hopkins'
poem 'God's Grandeur,' and Sam Keen's story of the peach-seed
monkey.

The Prodigal Son

11 And he said, 'There was a man who had two sons; 12 and the younger of them said to his father, "Father, give me the share of my property that falls to me." And he divided his living between them. 13 Not many days later, the younger son gathered all he had and took his journey into a far country, and there he squandered his property in loose living. 14 And when he had spent everything, a great famine arose in that country, and he began to be in want. 15 So he went and joined himself to one of the citizens of that country, who sent him into his fields to feed swine. 16 And he would gladly have fed on the pods that the swine ate; and no one gave him anything. 17 But when he came to himself he said, "How many of my father's hired servants have bread enough and to spare, but I perish here with hunger! 18 I will arise and go to my father, and I will say to him, 'Father, I have sinned against heaven and before you; 19 I am no longer worthy to be called your son; treat me as one of your hired servants.'" 20 And he arose and came to his father. But while he was yet at a distance, his father saw him and had compassion, and ran and embraced him and kissed him. 21 And the son said to him, "Father, I have sinned against heaven and before you; I am no longer worthy to be called your son." 22 But the father said to his servants, "Bring quickly the best robe, and put it on him; and put a ring on his hand, and shoes on his feet. 23 And bring the fatted calf and kill it, and let us eat and make merry; 24 for this my son was dead, and is alive again; he was lost, and is found." And they began to make merry.

25 'Now his elder son was in the fields; and as he came and drew near to the house, he heard music and dancing. 26 And he called one of the servants and asked what this meant. 27 And he said to him, "Your brother has come, and your father has killed the fatted calf, because he has received him safe and sound." 28 But he was angry and refused to go in. His father came out and entreated him, 29 but he answered his father, "Lo, these many years I have served you, and I never disobeyed your command; yet you never gave me a kid, that I might make merry with my friends. 30 But when this son of yours came, who has devoured

your living with harlots, you killed for him the fatted calf!" 31
And he said to him, "Son, you are always with me, and all that
is mine is yours. 32 It was fitting to make merry and be glad,
for this your brother was dead, and is alive; he was lost, and is
found." '

(Luke 15:11–32)

A parable is an extended metaphor. A parable is not an allegory,
where the meaning is extrinsic to the story, nor is it an example
story where, as in the story of the Good Samaritan, the total meaning
is within the story. Rather, as an extended metaphor, the meaning
is found only *within* the story itself although it is not exhausted *by*
that story. At the same time that a parable is an aesthetic whole and
hence demands rapt attention on itself and its configurations, it is
open-ended, expanding ordinary meaning so that from a careful analysis of the parable we learn a new thing, are shocked into a new awareness. *How* the new insight occurs is, of course, the heart of the matter;
it is enough to say at this point that the two dimensions – the ordinary
and the extraordinary – are related intricately *within* the confines of
the parable so that such 'God-talk' as we have in the Prodigal Son is
an existential, worldly, sensuous story of *human life*.

The shock, surprise, or revelatory aspect – the insight into
fatherly love – is carried in the parable of the Prodigal Son by the
radicalness of the imagery and action. This parable, like many others,
is economical, tense, riven with radical comparisons and disjunc-
tions. The comparisons are extreme; what is contrasted, however,
is not this world versus another world, but the radicalness of love,
faith, and hope *within* this world. The setting is worldly but the
orientation or 'frame' of the story is radical. The radical dimension
provides the context which disrupts the ordinary dimension and
allows us to see it anew as re-formed by God's extraordinary love.
What is 'seen,' however, is not something 'spiritual' (God's love 'in
itself,' whatever that would be), but the homely and familiar in a
new context – ordinary life lived in a new context, the context of
radical, unmerited love. That love – and God himself – are nowhere
directly mentioned in the story; the perception of divine love is
achieved through stretching the surface of the story with an extreme
imagery of hunger and feasting, rejection and acceptance, lost and
found, death and life.

The pattern of extreme contrasts runs throughout the entire parable, from the father's willingness to divide his property without question and the son's decision to take '*all* he had' and go into a '*far* country' where he '*squandered* his property in *loose* living' to the extraordinary developments upon the son's return. The imagery of life and death dominates the parable at its beginning, middle, and end: the most radical dichotomy sets the tone for the other extreme images. At the outset of the parable the son treats the father as if he were dead, for, as Günther Bornkamm mentions, a son has the right of disposal of property only after a father's death.[3] The extremism is also evident in such phrases as 'he had spent *everything*,' 'a *great* famine arose,' 'no one gave him *anything*.' His job, feeding swine, is of course the worst possible one since it brought him into direct contact with unclean animals; he, however, was so close to starvation he would gladly have eaten the swine's food. Verse 17 is the turning point of the parable, and, characteristically, it is an absolute about-face ('but he came to himself'); his repentance countenances no rationalizations. The surrealistic or 'absurd' part of the story, what makes it a parable, begins in earnest in verse 20, with the undignified and poignant image of the father spying the boy from a distance (how many times, we wonder, had he watched that road during those long months?) and running to embrace him (older Near Easterners did *not* run).[4] The 'compassion' of the father is expressed in the distinctive New Testament usage of a word that means 'love from the bowels.' When the boy starts to give his repentance speech exactly as rehearsed, the father cuts him short and changes the unspoken words to their opposite – the son is not to be considered a servant but an honored guest. The extraordinary love and graciousness of the father for the boy is entirely without grounding in anything the boy has done or said – even his repentance speech is cut short. Then in breathless succession more unmerited gifts are heaped upon the prodigal: the best robe (the ceremonial robe which in the East is a mark of high distinction), a ring (a signet ring is a sign of authority), shoes (a luxury worn only by free men, not slaves), a fatted calf (in a land where meat is rarely eaten). All of this happens because, and here the main imagery of the parable emerges again, the lost is found, the dead is alive. The latter part of the parable – the refusal and rejection by the elder son – is dealt with in the same way, through lavish, extraordinary, 'absurd' generosity.

One *could* paraphrase this parable in the theological assertion 'God's love knows no bounds,' but to do that would be to miss what the parable can do for our insight into such love. For what *counts* here is not extricating an abstract concept but precisely the opposite, delving into the details of the story itself, letting the metaphor do its job of revealing the new setting for ordinary life. It is the play of the radical images that does the job. If we want to talk about what this parable has to say about God, we must do so in terms that do not extrapolate from that moment when the father, waiting these many months, finally sees his son, and we must do so in terms that dig into the details *of* that moment. Thus the radical contrasts and the concrete images are not embellishments but are the meaning, for there is no way to the meaning except through them.

Dan Via talks about the 'in-meaning' and the 'through-meaning' of metaphors: meanings that are united inseparably as form and content, body and awareness. 'The human organism is a body that thinks, and in all thinking the mind unites with a figure-language – of its own devising.'[5] 'A body that thinks': this description of human life would satisfy Rubenstein and Keen, it is the assumption of all metaphorical language, and it is also basically and radically Christian. The modern post-Cartesian split of mind and body is radically anti-Christian; meaning and truth for human beings are embodied, hence *embodied language*, metaphorical language, is the most appropriate way – perhaps the only way – to suggest this meaning and truth. The multiplication table, and, we might add, the conceptual clarity of doctrinal creeds or theological propositions, are not *more* true for human beings than are the myth of the fall or the parable of the Prodigal Son. Metaphorical language is a mirror of our own constitution: the unity of body and soul, outer and inner, familiar and unfamiliar, known and unknown. Metaphorical language conveys meaning through the body of the world. It makes connections, sees resemblances, uniting body and soul – earthly, temporal, ordinary experience with its meaning. But the 'meaning' is not there to be read off conceptually; we only get at the meaning through the metaphor.

Metaphorical or imagistic language has the peculiar quality of both expressing and communicating at the same time. *Glossolalia*, speaking in strange tongues, expresses but does not communicate;

logical or highly conceptual language communicates precisely but is not highly expressive. Only metaphorical language, because it sets the familiar in a new context, does both – it can express more than the familiar and yet at the same time communicate, since it uses terms known to us. The kingdom (the unfamiliar) is a coin which a woman lost and found; it is a valuable pearl. *New* meaning is generated by making words mean more than they ordinarily do: this, in fact, is the definition of metaphor. But at the same time it is an entirely indirect mode. There are no explicit statements about God; everything is refracted through the earthly metaphor or story. Metaphor is, I believe, the heart of the parabolic tradition of religious reflection as contrasted with the more propositionally oriented tradition of regular or systematic theology.

The insistence on embodied language, on the indirection of metaphor, on the intimate relations of the ordinary and the extraordinary *within* the parable does not mean that 'nothing is said about God' in a parable and in theological reflection based on parables. But it does mean that we must be precise when we speak of *how* assertions are made about God in parables. They are made not in direct propositions but with what Philip Wheelwright calls 'soft focus' or 'assertorial lightness.'* This is the case because, as Wheelwright says, 'the plain fact is that not all facts are plain.'

> 'The Lord whose oracle is at Delphi,' said Heraclitus referring to Apollo the god and symbol of wisdom, 'neither speaks nor conceals but gives signs'. . . .There are meanings of high, sometimes of very high importance, which cannot be stated in terms strictly defined. . . .Plain speech may sometimes have conceptual exactitude, but it will be inaccurate with respect to the new thing that one wants to say, the freshly imagined experience that one wants to describe and communicate.[6]

Such 'assertions' can *only* be made lightly or in soft focus. Thus parables are not only, as I have maintained, a deformation of ordinary

---

* See also Michael Polanyi's distinction between 'focal' and 'subsidiary' awareness in Chapter One of *The Tacit Dimension* (Garden City: Doubleday, 1966). In this distinction, the parable and our existential situation it depicts would claim our focal awareness while what the parable tells us of God would claim our subsidiary awareness.

life by placing that life in the context of the new and extraordinary, but they also tell us, though indirectly, something about the new and extraordinary context. The parables make ontological as well as existential 'assertions' – they tell us something about God as well as something about our life – but the assertions about God are made lightly, indirectly, and cannot be extricated finally and completely from the story which expresses or, better, 'images' them.*

God's Grandeur

The world is charged with the grandeur of God.
   It will flame out, like shining from shook foil;
   It gathers to a greatness, like the ooze of oil
Crushed. Why do men then now not reck his rod?
Generations have trod, have trod, have trod;
   And all is seared with trade; bleared, smeared with toil;
   And wears man's smudge and shares man's smell: the soil
Is bare now, nor can foot feel, being shod.

And for all this, nature is never spent;
   There lives the dearest freshness deep down things;
And though the last lights off the black West went
   Oh, morning, at the brown brink eastward, springs –
Because the Holy Ghost over the bent
   World broods with warm breast and with ah! bright wings.[7]

    At first glance this poem by Gerard Manley Hopkins seems miles removed from the parable of the Prodigal Son: it appears to be 'about' God, or at least about nature, rather than about human life.

---

* Richard Kroner points out that Jesus' parables are not symbols since they do not point to something other than themselves. 'A symbol is something that signifies something else. . . .Most of the parables symbolize the idea of the kingdom of God. But is this idea a symbol itself? Of course, it has a metaphorical meaning, but this meaning no longer symbolizes any other meaning or fact; it is therefore not a symbol, it is a religious image. The truth, expressed by the image of the kingdom of God, cannot be fully grasped by means of thought. Therefore the image is not a real symbol at all; it does not symbolize any concept; it "images" the mystery. . . .The religious image stands for itself, or for the thing it means' (*The Religious Function of Imagination* [New Haven: Yale University Press, 1941], pp. 40–41).

But note that it speaks of God *only* in his grandeur, that is, it speaks of him only sacramentally through his effects – the *world* is charged with the *grandeur* of God – and it speaks of nature and human beings inextricably involved with each other, ecologically, symbiotically united – nature wears our smudge and shares our smell. The theme of the poem is the renewal of the world, a renewal that is not merely natural but is from the providential, life-giving hand of God. As with the Prodigal Son we discover this theme only *through* the metaphors of the poem, only through its *own* intrinsic details.

'God's Grandeur' is of course a sonnet, with the first eight lines laying out the situation and the sestet giving the resolution, and as with most sonnets the last two lines hold a special revelatory surprise. It is a highly intricate poem and we can do no more than suggest a few of the intricacies, but it is important to indicate some of them, for my thesis is that the *details* are the meaning of the poem.

1.1　　'Charged' suggests the modern image of electricity (and more generally of potency) but the word also has overtones of responsibility as in 'charged with a responsibility'; therefore the image is both impersonal and personal.

1.2　　'Flame out' picks up the electricity image from 1.1 and also implies movement outward, the enveloping power of flame to consume all. In his notes on the poem, Hopkins writes of 'shook foil': 'I mean foil in the sense of leaf or tinsel . . . Shaken gold-foil gives off broad glares like sheet lightning and also, and *this is true of nothing else*, owing to its zigzag dents and creasings and network of small many cornered facets, a sort of fork lightning too.'[8] The image of shook foil is one of glory, brilliance, light, and power: God's grandeur in nature is unmistakable, *obvious*.

1.3　　The outward shining movement is now contracted, it 'gathers to a greatness' like the 'ooze of oil,' and a shift of tone is implied in the ambiguous sound of the 'o's' here.

1.4　　Crushed: golden spurts of oil spatter out. The grandeur of God is so obvious it could hit you in the eye. So why do men not see it, why do they not 'reck his rod' – a phrase that recalls the 'charged' of 1.1. The responsibility of nature to show forth God's grandeur is mirrored in man's responsibility to *see* the grandeur in nature.

11.5–8 The topic changes to men and what they have done to nature and the new subject is carried by the mechanical image of the treadmill ('have trod, have trod, have trod') and the nasty 's' sounds – seared, smeared, smudge, shares, smell, soil, shod. Here are some nice ecological and anti-pollution overtones in 1877: man cannot *feel* the earth or, by implication, perceive God in nature, since he wears shoes.

1.9 The sestet opens with the renewal of nature. The power for renewal appears to be within nature – the instress or pressure of God comes immanently, not as a *deus ex machina* but from the incredible resources of renewal with which God has endowed the world.

1.11 'Last lights off the black West' envisions a total catastrophe, a Hiroshima of civilization, the setting of the sun for the last time.

1.12 The reversal begins: a new day, a gradual lessening of 'black' to 'brown,' a new morning 'springs' – a lively physical movement, and also a new spring following the winter (a suggestion of the cycle of fertility-nature cults).

11.13–14 All the foregoing happens *because* of the Holy Ghost (it is not a fertility cult or an entirely immanent occurrence). Here in the image of the dove, as solicitous as a mother bird with her warm breast, recalling Genesis 1 in 'broods,' the Holy Ghost manifests the power of a second creation carried by the exclamation, 'with ah! bright wings.' It is not just the warmth of the nest of creation but the glory and unexpected possibilities implied in the image of the bird's wings rising radiantly against the rising sun. These images of radiance recall, of course, the opening images of the poem and bring us back to the grandeur of God shining in the world.

It is useful to recall that Hopkins was a follower of Duns Scotus, with his skepticism about the range of theological reason. Nowhere in this poem does Hopkins talk directly *about God*: the language is imagistic and metaphorical at all times – electricity, flame, tinfoil,

oil, morning, dove, wings. There is no way to the 'theology,' if you will, except through the poetry, and this is not, I believe, just precious aestheticism. For, just to take that last metaphor of the bird and plumb its intrinsic meanings – creation, rebirth, nest, comfort, care for the *bent* world, and finally *bright* wings – is a lesson in the appropriateness of metaphorical theological language for a human being – 'a body that thinks.' Hopkins' poem is an existential, sensuous story of human beings in relation to God, a panoramic story of the violations of God's world by them and God's renewal of it. What one 'gets' from this story, this poem, is not new information that can be catalogued but *new insight* into what we might call the gracious power of God in the world or better, his powerful graciousness. A deep probing of the metaphors of the poem puts us in touch with the graciousness of God's power as it impinges on and renews our familiar world; we feel we understand somewhat better, in terms that matter to us – personal, worldly, concrete terms – what such a notion might mean.

The Peach-Seed Monkey

Once upon a time when there were still Indians, Gypsies, bears, and bad men in the woods of Tennessee where I played and, more important still, there was no death, a promise was made to me. One endless summer afternoon my father sat in the eternal shade of a peach tree, carving on a seed he had picked up. With increasing excitement and covetousness I watched while, using a skill common to all omnipotent creators, he fashioned a small monkey out of the seed. All of my vagrant wishes and desires disciplined themselves and came to focus on that peach-seed monkey. If only I could have it, I would possess a treasure which could not be matched in the whole cosmopolitan town of Maryville! What status, what identity, I would achieve by owning such a curio! Finally I marshaled my nerve and asked if I might have the monkey when it was finished (on the sixth day of creation). My father replied, 'This one is for your mother, but I will carve you one some day.'

Days passed, then weeks and, finally, years, and the someday on which I was to receive the monkey did not arrive. In truth,

I forgot all about the peach-seed monkey. Life in ambience of my father was exciting, secure, and colorful. He did all of those things for his children a father can do, not the least of which was merely delighting in their existence. One of the lasting tokens I retained of the measure of his dignity and courage was the manner in which, with emphysema sapping his energy and eroding his future, he continued to wonder, to struggle, and to grow.

In the pure air and dry heat of an Arizona afternoon on the summer before the death of God, my father and I sat under a juniper tree. I listened as he wrestled with the task of taking the measure of his success and failure in life. There came a moment of silence that cried out of testimony. Suddenly I remembered the peach-seed monkey, and I heard the right words coming from myself to fill the silence: 'In all that is important you have never failed me. With one exception, you kept the promises you made to me – you never carved me that peach-seed monkey.'

Not long after this conversation I received a small package in the mail. In it was a peach-seed monkey and a note which said: 'Here is the monkey I promised you. You will notice that I broke one leg and had to repair it with glue. I am sorry I didn't have time to carve a perfect one.'

Two weeks later my father died. He died only at the end of his life.[9]

When we move from Hopkins' poem to Sam Keen's story of a peach-seed monkey, we seem to be in another world again. There is no grandeur of God crackling and flaming here, but an atmosphere which is described as *post-Christian* and *death of God*. Keen sees no possibility of using the metaphors and stories and myths of the tradition: he must start with his own story and see if from that 'there is anything in my experience which gives it unity, depth, density, dignity, meaning, and value – which makes graceful freedom possible.'[10] This is his central question and I do not think it wrong or inappropriate when dealing with Keen's radically personal and subjective, anti-traditionalist, anti-God-talk story of the peach-seed monkey to keep in mind the compassion of the father for the son in the parable of the Prodigal Son and the warmth and bright wings of the dove brooding over the bent world in Hopkins' poem. In all three cases, I believe, we are concerned with human confidence in the foundations of being *as told in the human story*.

Keen has himself analyzed his story of the peach-seed monkey. He says that for him the peach-seed monkey is a symbol for 'all the promises which were made to me and the energy and care which nourished and created me as a human being.'[11] It became for him translucent to another reality – 'my sense of the basic trustworthiness of the world and my consequent freedom to commit myself to action.'[12] He can become through the story a receiver and a maker of promises; this gives a unity of past, present, and future for him and hence gives him a 'story,' an identity. Keen does not believe the peach-seed monkey is only his story; one like it lies in each person's biography and, as he says, 'in the depth of each man's biography lies the story of all men.'[13] In the depths of this story of the peach-seed monkey lies Keen's sense of the holy and the sacred: the basic solicitude of life which makes graceful freedom possible. Keen would not call this God-talk, nor shall we; but whatever it is, it is certainly in the same tradition as the Prodigal Son and 'God's Grandeur.' Keen's story is not of the same calibre as the others. The fact that he added an 'explanation' is the giveaway: the peach-seed monkey is really a symbol, not a metaphor – that is, it 'stands for' something (and he tells us what that something is). The correlation in a symbol is much tighter than in a metaphor – one thing stands for another thing – and it loses the multilayered, rich, and always partly ambiguous or 'soft' focus of a metaphor. The fact that Keen sees his life as a story and events in it within a context of graciousness reveals his sensitivity to the necessity of dealing with religious insight indirectly, but his straight talk *about* the meaning of the story of the peach-seed monkey suggests a failure of nerve and a wish to take shortcuts. His analysis makes the story little more than an illustration of what he obviously can say more directly in discursive language. But the desire is there in Keen and in many others for a secular, indirect, low-key way of dealing with the graciousness experienced in ordinary life.

The language of a people is their sense of reality; we can live only within the confines of our language. If that language is one-dimensional, as Herbert Marcuse puts it, if it is jargon, the jargon of technocracy, of Madison Avenue, of politics – or of theology – then we lead one-dimensional lives, meaningless lives, lives within language that has ceased to express our depths for it is not capable of expressing anything but the limits of what we *already* know and feel. It is no longer open to or suggestive of any reality beyond itself, and hence we have no means of renewing ordinary life and language, of seeing it in new contexts. Our ability to express the deeper dimensions of human existence is determined by the metaphorical aliveness of our language, and that language in turn is controlled by the vision of reality we hold. The teller of the parable of the Prodigal Son, Hopkins, and, to some extent, Keen beheld a vision of reality that demanded a breakthrough beyond one-dimensional, univocal language – it demanded metaphor, for such is always the route out of established meaning to new meaning; and metaphor in turn became the proper vehicle for the expression and communication of what they beheld – it is the language for 'a body that thinks.'

For many of us the language of the Christian tradition is no longer authoritative; no longer revelatory; no longer metaphorical; no longer meaningful. Much of it has become tired clichés, one-dimensional, univocal language. When this happens, it means that theological reflection is faced with an enormous task – the task of embodying it anew. This will not happen, I believe, through systematic theology, for systematic theology is second-level language, language which orders, arranges, explicates, makes precise the first-order revelatory, metaphorical language. How the renovation of basic Christian language will take place will not, I suspect, be unlike the 'way' we see in the tradition of religious reflection we have been analyzing. It will be through the search for new metaphors – poems, stories, even lives – which will 'image' to us, in our total existential unity, the compassion of the father, the bright wings of the bird, the trustworthiness of a world in which parents keep promises to their children.

Contemporary poems, novels, and autobiographies can serve as imaginative re-creations, 'deformations,' of the old, allowing us to see the old in a new setting and thus to see it anew. What is at stake here is not simply the renewal of Christian symbols and traditional language – it is not the problem of translating what old symbols 'say' into contemporary language – but the more basic hermeneutical task of understanding the creative imagination as that which uniquely allows us to see and say the conceptually imperceivable and inexpressible. Much of the present essay will be an attempt to get a sighting on this agonizingly difficult task, what we could call in other words the relationship between parable and theology – the word of address and words oriented toward serving the hearing of that address. Although the way from parable to theology, Robert Funk says, is 'circuitous and tortuous,'[14] still the language of the imagination was at our beginning, and in spite of the rocky path, it will be always an ingredient in all our theology or we will abdicate our task – the service of helping God's word to be heard.

It appears that history has brought theological language full circle: having begun with the poetry of parable, metaphor, simile, and aphorism, it seems that theology is being thrust back upon the language of its infancy. The reason may be that just as faith could not be presupposed then, it cannot be presupposed now. In such a context the redeeming word must lay its own foundation: by its power as word it must be able to bring that world into being in which faith is possible, indeed necessary. Only then is it possible for theology to extrapolate conceptually from faith's experience of the world as redeemed. If, in the intervening centuries, theology has grown less and less solicitous of its ownmost origin, it is now being forced to renew itself at its source – or perish.[15]

Forms of Religious Reflection
and the Traditon

Amos Wilder has written that 'the language of a people is its fate.'

> Any human language represents a special kind of order superimposed upon existence. Generations live in it as a habitat in which they are born and die. Outside of it is nescience. . . .Perhaps one can say that nothing affects the significance of human existence more than the range and resource of our articulation, vocabulary, syntax and discourse.[1]

It is almost a common assumption now that human beings *are* linguistic – this, and not our reason (understood abstractly, non-linguistically) is what is most distinctive about us. We are the ones who speak (reason or conceptualization is dependent on linguistic symbolization), who name all things and thus give order to our world and give ourselves a past and a future. George Steiner has written:

> That articulate speech should be the line dividing man from the myriad forms of animate being, that speech should define man's singular eminence above the silence of the plant and the grunt of the beast . . . is classic doctrine well before Aristotle. . . . Possessed of speech, possessed by it, the word having chosen the grossness and infirmity of man's condition for its own compelling life, the human person has broken free from the great silence of matter. Or, to use Ibsen's image: struck with the hammer, the insensate ore has begun to sing.[2]

It is not only a philosopher such as Martin Heidegger who speaks of language as 'the house of being,' but almost universal opinion that human beings are linguistic through and through.* If one notices the way an animal looks at something as against the way we do, the difference is language – we can do something other than smell things and decide whether they are good to eat or dangerous. We can remember, generalize, hope, particularize, compare, contrast, wish, and so on, all because the object before us is also a 'word,' a symbol, that can enter into all sorts of relations with other symbols.

Moreover, we have become highly self-conscious about language. As Iris Murdoch says, 'We can no longer take language for granted as a medium of communication. Its transparency is gone. We are like people who for a long time looked out of a window without noticing the glass – and then one day began to notice this too.'³ While our self-consciousness about language is in many ways a contemporary phenomenon, the Judaic-Christian tradition, being strongly verbal, has always been self-conscious about language. Contrasted with nature cults, mystic religions, liturgical and ritualistic traditions, Judaism and Christianity are 'logos' religions: human beings are constituted by the Word as well as by words, or by the Word as made known to them through words. The Hebraic tradition is not visual but aural: Hear the word of the Lord, saith the prophet. And Protestant theology is agonizingly, painfully verbal and linguistic. Since the eighteenth century and particularly since the historical and biblical criticism of the late nineteenth century, Protestant theology has been nothing if not linguistic – a battle over words and what they mean.

Theologians during this entire century have been consumed by the problem of the Word and its relation to words: Karl Barth's thundering Word, plunging us all into biblical repetition or holy

---

* We might take only two quite disparate corroborations of this point. W. M. Urban says: 'Language is the last and deepest problem of the philosophic mind. This is true whether we approach reality through life or through intellect and science. All life, as Henry James has said, comes back to the question of our speech, the medium through which we communicate. Life as it is merely lived is senseless. It is perhaps conceivable that we may have a direct apprehension or intuition of life, but the meaning of life can neither be apprehended nor expressed except in language of some kind. Such expression or communication is part of the life process itself.' And the *Upanishads*: 'If there were no speech, neither right nor wrong would be known, neither true nor false, neither the pleasant nor the unpleasant. Speech makes us understand all this. Meditate on speech.' Both statements are from Urban's *Language and Reality: The Philosophy of Language and the Principles of Symbolism* (New York: Macmillan, 1939), p. 21.

silence; Rudolf Bultmann's demythologizing program, highly sus-
picious of symbolic and mythological language, opting instead for the
likewise metaphorical language (even though it was not recognized as
such) of the early Heidegger; Paul Tillich's extensive work on symbolic language; the 'new hermeneutic,' which is linguisticality epito-
mized, and so on. Like it or not, ours is a linguistic era; the word
may be dying, as Marshall McLuhan claims, or debased, as George
Steiner asserts, but all fields are obsessed by it, most especially those
closest to religious studies – literary criticism, anthropology, and
philosophy.

Moreover, a particular kind of language has emerged as of crucial
importance. In the post–Cartesian world there was a trend toward
scientific precision in language, but there has been for some time
now a gradual reawakening to what is lost in language where 'sign'
replaces symbol. In such language the world dwindles unnecessarily.
The life story of the philosopher Ludwig Wittgenstein is an interesting case in point here: he moved from a position where each word
points to or pictures a thing to one in which there are many 'language
games'; that is, language does many things, some of which cannot
be verified empirically. To put the matter over–simply, those con-
vinced of the centrality of imagistic language to all human discourse
will say that language in *all* areas (the sciences as well as religion
and the arts) does not only describe – it also, especially when it is
trying to speak of the new, evokes and intimates. Children's language
is highly imagistic, but scientists also use models to serve as metaphors for what they cannot describe directly. Poets and religious
folk need not be embarrassed by the indirection and metaphorical
nature of their language – all profound human discourse is of such
a character as attested to by a mighty company: Plato, Augustine,
Thomas Aquinas, Barth, Tillich, Whitehead, Heidegger, not to mention Jesus and Paul. Either we accept the necessity of metaphorical
language for what might be called 'the mysteries of life' or we sink
into silence, or speaking in tongues, or a kind of literal-mindedness
which is very difficult for a contemporary, educated person to
defend. Augustine realized that it was either silence or metaphor,
either the blinding Light of the rare mystical moment or talking in
terms of loving 'light and melody and fragrance and food and
embrace when I love my God.'[4] Edwyn Bevan makes a similar point:

There is the old story of someone born blind having explained to him what the colour scarlet was by his being told that it was like the sound of a trumpet. Whether that was a happy analogy or not, it is plain that the only possible way in which a person born blind could be given any information regarding colour is by the use of some things within his experience, as symbols working through analogy.[5]

What we have been talking about – the metaphorical nature of the language of revelation and insight – has been called elsewhere the hermeneutical circle. The days of supposing we are free of finite limitations, of supposing that we have some direct access to 'Truth,' that there might be words that correspond to 'what is,' that 'clear and distinct ideas' can be many or very interesting – such a time is over (if it ever existed except in the most rationalistic circles). The most sensitive and perceptive poets, theologians, philosophers, and scientists have always known better. What we have and all that we have is the grid or screen provided by this metaphor and by that metaphor. The metaphor *is* the thing, or at least the only access that we highly relative and limited beings have to it. That such a situation leaves us feeling uneasy is an understatement. We grasp after certainty, after direct access to the way things 'really are.' As Frederick Ferré asks, 'Is not the religious believer entitled to care about what reality is "really" like behind the unmovable veil of his images?'[6]* But caring does not of itself bring satisfaction; the acceptance of the necessity of metaphorical language means also the acceptance of risk, of openendedness, of skepticism,† To live in this

---

* 'Surely it is meaningful for each man to *hope* that the metaphors he adopts as his own, for the representations of what no mind can know unclad in some sort of imagery, are not without a basis of similarity (could he but compare them) in the referent to which they inadequately point. But all that he can *know* is the extent to which he and the religious community of which he is a part finds them relatively adequate and reliable when times of testing come. And no more, after all, is really needed in this life. The rest he must hold only as a hope and a constant reminder of his finitude as knower. The rest, as the metaphors of great tradition would interpret it for us, he must be content to "leave in God's hands" ' (Frederick Ferré, 'Metaphors, Models, and Religion,' *Soundings*, 51 [1968], 345).

† Relativism and skepticism are not simply the lot of religion. Ian G. Barbour, in the conclusion to a book on models and paradigms in religion and science, makes a telling remark about the ground they share: '. . . science is not as objective, nor religion as subjective, as the view dominant among philosophers of religion has held.

language milieu is to live in faith and hope, not in the certainty of knowledge, but it is also, not incidentally, where Jesus' parables, with their images and stories, insist we must live.'

The Near Tradition: Contemporary Theology

The problem of the directness and certainty of our words about the word of God is clearly seen in the giants of contemporary theology, Karl Barth and Rudolf Bultmann. Both Barth and Bultmann, for all their differences, focus on preaching the word of God to today's people. *The* question is: How can our words be appropriate to today's people so that God's action can take place through them? To say, as Gerhard Ebeling does, that hermeneutic is the whole of theology may sound like esoteric reductionism, but when one realizes that 'hermeneutic' means translating the word spoken in the Bible into the word for today it seems neither esoteric nor reductionistic; it is simply what theology – that helpmeet of the preacher – always has been about when it has been about its proper business. *How* this translation is to occur is what divides Barth from Bultmann, and divides what I have called intermediary theology from both of them. It is the *form* of religious or theological reflection that is crucial.

For Barth that form must be an *objective* spelling out of the word of God in Scripture, resulting in a dogmatics or system of theology. We are the hearers of the word, a word that God spoke in primal history and which determines secular or ordinary history. God alone sets the conditions for hearing and the theologian need not trouble him- or herself about contemporary idioms or events. It is not that Barth is unconcerned with concrete events of contemporary life – his own actions during the two World Wars and in relation to Eastern Europe have revealed his deep personal concern – but they are not determinative for hearing and responding to the gospel.

Man the knower plays a crucial role throughout science. Scientific models are products of creative analogical imagination. Data are theory-laden; comprehensive theories are resistant to falsification; and there are no rules for paradigm choice. . . .I see a difference of degree between science and religion rather than an absolute contrast' (*Myths, Models and Paradigms: A Comparative Study in Science and Religion* [New York: Harper and Row, 1974], p. 171).

God's action in Jesus Christ – the man judged and saved in our place – creates its own possibility of response and the job of the theologian is to meticulously spell out that action, not to worry about its results.

For Bultmann the form of translation must be a *subjective* appropriation of the good news in Scripture, issuing in a critique of the mythological categories of the New Testament in contrast to perennial 'existential' categories of human self-understanding. Whereas Barth focuses on the word of God to which faith responds, Bultmann focuses on faith that responds to the word. Bultmann moves inward and thus hopes to overcome cultural and historical relativity – we no longer understand ourselves and our world in nonscientific, mythological terms – because subjectively human beings are always the same. 'Inauthentic' and 'unfulfilled' existence is the same for our biblical brothers and sisters as for us, and in fact, their myths were *about* inauthentic versus authentic existence. Bultmann translates the myths not into metaphysics (which is still quasi–objective) but into existentialist categories. Thus we find his solution to the Kantian limit – there is no way to talk about things 'out there' – in terms of limiting the good news to the *pro nobis*; one does not talk about the New Testament as *Historie* (objective, factual history) but as *Geschichte* (the meaning of the events for the persons who encounter them).

It may be an oversimplification to put the distinction between Barth and Bultmann in terms of objective versus subjective; yet it is, I believe, not only accurate but essential, for this is the shoal on which they founder. If the question is *how* the people of today are to hear the good news, what *form* theological reflection should take to help this to happen, it seems to me that we are driven back, in a religion such as Christianity that has put all its eggs into the verbal basket, to the nature of language itself. If one takes metaphor to be the crucial constitutive of language, the subjective–objective split is false.

Biblical language, as we shall see shortly, is not of the subjective-objective variety but speaks to us deeply, as does poetry, precisely because it overcomes the split, or better yet does not recognize it. It is metaphorical language, language which in this image and in that unites the concrete and the abstract, the sensuous and the mental, the particular and the general, the subjective and the objective. How can one say that a parable of Jesus or the ancient image of the body of Christ is one or the other? Those categories are not significant. It is assumed, rather, that the familiar (Bultmann's 'pre-understanding,' if you will) – common experiences and everyday words – is the means for grasping the unfamiliar, but the connections between these two dimensions are rung in such a way (the way poets ring them) that the strange and unfamiliar (Barth's action of God on behalf of his people, if you will) breaks apart and renovates the familiar. The significant categories are not subjective and objective, but old and new (old wineskins and new wine, the old man Adam and the new man Jesus, old creation and new creation, death and life) – accepted patterns and new interpretations, clichés and new meaning, old facts and new insight into them. Metaphorical language, as the language of 'a body that thinks,' knows no subjective-objective split; the split, if you will, comes at the point of 'what is' and 'what might be.'

This is basically what I want to say. The way we *hear* the good news is not through some mysterious process outside of anything we have ever encountered (the way Barth seems to believe the word of God comes to a person), nor does it require a special translation into subjective existentialist categories (the way Bultmann believes). The meaning of the gospel is generated through metaphor, through words which we 'know' but which are now put into a new context so that we see 'what is' in the light of 'what might be,' the ordinary emerges shaped by a new context. Thus we *move*, through metaphor, *to* meaning; metaphor is a *motion* from here to there. If we say, as I would want to, that Jesus of Nazareth is par excellence the metaphor of God, we mean that his familiar, mundane story is the *way*, the indirect but necessary way, from here to there. It also means that we take, as metaphor does, the 'body,' not as flesh alone but as the totality of human experiencing in the familiar and the mundane, as the way to God. The process, therefore, is by no means mainly intellectual; on the contrary, metaphoric meaning, insisting as it always does on a physical base, is inclusive meaning which overcomes the distinctions of mind and body, reason and feeling, subjective and objective. Another way to say this is that metaphoric meaning is a *process*, not a momentary, static insight; it operates like a story, moving from here to there, from 'what is' to 'what might be.'

And the discrete metaphors of the New Testament – the parables, the passion story, the images and anecdotes – were and are for us today *good* metaphors for helping us to hear the good news. They are inseparable from their content – there is no way of getting at the 'essence' of Christianity apart from them; and they are both so common and so basic to human experience – stories of fathers and sons, images of blood and bread and bodies – that they invite prolonged contemplation and reward the reader with inexhaustible insight. They are not, however, sacrosanct or exclusivistic. There is no reason, given this understanding of metaphor, why other stories, metaphors, and images ought not also be forms of reflection that serve to aid us in hearing the word of God. And yet, because form and content are inextricably linked, there will always be a certain priority to the biblical forms. These forms, these metaphors, were reached for in a time nearer to the event which marks the basis of Christianity and there is no way of preserving the 'content' of these metaphors apart from the form. As John Dillenberger says, there is no way *around* formulations of the past, only a way *through* them, getting in on their intentionality.[7]

To see the form of theological reflection in metaphorical terms takes the Kantian limits seriously. There is no way *around* metaphors, neither an objective nor a subjective route, neither a leaving it all to God as Barth does nor a demythologizing of poetic language into existential categories as Bultmann does. We cannot accept either the subjective cul-de-sac of Bultmann (all that can be said of God must be said in terms of my own transformed life) or the objective presumption of Barth (his peculiar epistemology which recognizes the Kantian limits in all instances but one, the biblical revelation). Neither Barth nor Bultmann recognizes fully the radical limits of our language and the possibilities for dealing with those limits in metaphorical language. Bultmann's failings here are obvious (Robert Funk says that Bultmann 'appears not to have a poetic bone in his body'[8]), for apparently he believed he had found a way around imagistic language, a means of direct access, with the existential categories of Martin Heidegger. Barth knew better – he knew that all religious language is necessarily analogical – but in his stress on biblical language and his refusal to take seriously any other language, whether philosophical, literary, or anthropological, he, at least implicitly, placed a premium on *one* language and hence has fed the appetites of the literal-minded for a privileged and direct vocabulary.*

In choosing to look at the failure of Barth and Bultmann to take seriously the necessity of metaphorical language as well as its potential for insight, we are suggesting *types* of escape from the limitations and special properties of imagistic language, one that is 'objective' and the other that is 'subjective.' These classifications would need many qualifications to do justice to Barth and Bultmann, both of whom were far more sophisticated in their use of language than these typologies would suggest. They do not fit the types precisely, and neither would their followers. Moreover, the classic tradition in Christian theology has been continually and painfully aware of the limits of language and the necessity of imagistic language. One has only to think of Augustine's awareness in the *Confessions* of the agonies of saying anything of God, Thomas's extensive work on analogy, Calvin's notion of the 'accommodation' of God to the limits of human language, Coleridge's treatment of the primary and secondary imagination, Kierkegaard's method of indirect communication, Tillich's work on symbol, and so on to get a sense of the richness of the tradition with regard to the language of the imagination.

The point in our brief analysis is only to underscore the peculiar way in which the contemporary crisis of language – our acknowledgment of the window glass, as Iris Murdoch puts it – has both elevated the importance of metaphorical language and, on the part of theologians as well as of others, made us painfully aware of its limitations, so much aware that the desire to escape is at times irresistible. But the Bible offers us no solace here, for it is a storehouse of the language of the imagination.

---

* That Barth does appreciate the indirect, metaphoric language of the New Testament is evident in this comment of his on parables: 'Let us consider the view of life which is expressed in the *parables* in the synoptic Gospels. . . .Is it not the simple way in which the kingdom of heaven is compared to the world? . . . and then follows regularly a picture of social life which in itself discloses nothing heavenly whatever. Not the moral world, nor the Christian, nor any theoretical and postulated world is described, but simply the world as one finds it. . . .The parables are pictures from life as it *is*, pictures that mean something' (*The Word of God and the Word of Man*, trans. Douglas Horton [New York: Harper and Row, 1951], pp. 303, 306).

The Far Tradition: The New Testament

'Story' is perhaps the least complicated way of approaching that storehouse of imagistic language. 'Everyone loves a good story.' It is fortunate for Christianity that this is true. But the relations between the story form and Christianity are much more complex, for in a crucial sense Christianity provided the impetus for storytelling, at least for telling stories of a particular kind. Erich Auerbach in his magnificent book *Mimesis* credits Christianity with introducing into Western letters a type of story which, as he says, is 'fraught with background.'[9] I would call it the story as extended metaphor. In contrast to Homer's stories which 'take place' right before the eyes, so to speak, and hence are full of surface detail and leisurely description, the stories of the Judaic-Christian tradition, from Abraham's sacrifice of Isaac to Peter's denial, take place in both the foreground and background; more precisely, the background is the context, the new and strange context, for the foreground of ordinary life. The pregnant silences in the Abraham story; the absence of detail and the economy of language; the momentous decisions embodied in simple, everyday discourse; the dialogue form giving an immediacy and vividness to the stories – these are the elements that 'work' the metaphor for us. They are not 'just stories,' but stories that mean more than such stories usually mean – after all, there have been other tales of human sacrifice and denial. These stories 'mean' more because they are metaphors. Specific literary devices concentrate attention, heighten involvement and the sense of immediacy, control diffusion and 'comic relief.' The focus in both of these stories is on the individual, both the individual *in* the story (Abraham and Peter) and the individual who reads the story. The sense of drama is high, for momentous decisions are being made, and the reader feels that he or she could well be that confronted human being.

The story, then, not any story but the story pregnant with meaning, the story as extended metaphor, is the *key* form of the New Testament. The only original literary genre in the New Testament is the gospel, which is, of course, such a story par excellence, the story of victory over death. Within the gospels are many small gospels – the parables, anecdotes, healings, teachings of Jesus –

which in nugget form also image the good news. The gospels and parables are not histories but reenactments of good news – dramatic narratives that 'say' the same thing that the big story, the story of Jesus' passion, death, and resurrection says. Amos Wilder in his excellent study of the literary forms of the New Testament, *The Language of the Gospel*, highlights the centrality of the story.

> The narrative mode is uniquely important in Christianity. . . .A Christian can confess his faith wherever he is, and without his Bible, just by telling a story or a series of stories. . . .Perhaps the special character of the stories of the New Testament lies in the fact that they are not told for themselves, that they are not only about other people, but that they are always about us. They locate us in the very midst of the great story and plot of all time and space, and therefore relate us to the great dramatist and story teller, God himself.[10]

Other literary forms of the New Testament – poem, prayer, confession, sermon, parable – all have strong narrative elements. The poetry of the New Testament, such as the Magnificat (Luke 1:46–55), is personal and responsive, focused on deliverance, and concrete and commonplace in its imagery. The confession of Paul, the first Christian autobiography, is a story told to manifest the good news – spare in form, honed to reveal in his own life the power of God's love. A Christian autobiography ought to be a metaphor of God's action, and even Paul's 'boasting' is for precisely that purpose. What cannot be conceptualized – the mysteriousness of God's love – can perhaps be made manifest through the story of one's own life. The sermon, such as Peter's sermon in Acts 2, is, of course, a recounting of the story of Jesus, crucified and risen. Finally, the parable, about which we will have much more to say, is perhaps the purest biblical form of the story as extended metaphor, for the parables of Jesus are unique in their extraordinary ability to embrace the transcendent within the economic, vivid, immediate stories of human, very human beings.

In all these instances, we have the common, ordinary language and images of the people used in new ways. Words such as blood, water, seed, bread, coins, sheep, and so on are used in the various literary genres of the New Testament as metaphors; that is, the 'dictionary' meanings of these words are given, as Owen Barfield would say, a 'speaker's meaning,' old words have taken on new meaning, the familiar has been given a new context so that new meaning is generated.[11] There are no 'technical' words in the New Testament, no words with special meanings; there are only words which have been made to mean more than they usually mean. This is only to say, of course, that, as Wilder puts it, 'the New Testament writings are in large part works of the imagination, loaded, charged and encrusted with every kind of figurative resource and invention.'[12] This may be blasphemy to the literal-minded; but it is fortunate that the New Testament writers were endowed with rich imaginations, for otherwise the New Testament would hold little chance of being revelatory.

What the New Testament writers apprehended in Jesus of Nazareth was a movement of the human – the human in its totality – beyond itself, in such a way that the totality of human life was itself re-created, and they did their best to suggest this apprehension through a variety of metaphors. Like their forefathers who apprehended holistically – and like poets of all times – the 'poets' of the New Testament saw something unfamiliar and strange coming clear to them in and through the mundanity of a human life. They saw the word of God coming to them through the events and sayings and stories of the man Jesus. They *saw* it that way and reported it that way, not stripping the husk from the kernel or translating it into general existentialist terms or systematizing it into statements about God, but following the way it had come to them. What began to come clear to them through the life and death of Jesus, that basic metaphor, became the touchstone for creating hundreds of other metaphors – old and new Adam, bread and wine, lost and found, free and slave, water and Spirit – which also, they hoped, would evoke the remarkable thing they believed had occurred in and through the life of Jesus. Because they are real metaphors there is no way of testing them against some abstract assertions – and the New Testament writers did not construct a theology of the nature of God or the person and work of Jesus Christ (though such assertions are implicit in these metaphors, as assertions are always implicit in metaphors) – but they can and ought to be juxtaposed to the central metaphor, the life and death of Jesus. This will not 'prove' they are adequate, but it will give us some hints whether or not they are. It will also, of course, serve as the touchstone for all other metaphors – images and stories – in all ages, including our own, which would seek to point to what is central in the Christian faith.

Metaphorical Language and Theological Reflection

New Testament language, then, and its principal form – the story, both as parable and as the story of Jesus – is metaphorical. If this is so, what are the implications for theology? What, for instance, ought the theologian to do with the New Testament stories? Ought he or she to abstract themes from the stories in rational, conceptual language and systematize the themes?

This is, in fact, what constitutes a great deal of theology. I am not attempting to negate the legitimacy or necessity of this enterprise, but I want to suggest that this is a task that depends upon and must constantly return to its source of new meaning, metaphorical language.* Serious attention to metaphorical language as the way to fund theology ought to change the way theological reflection is carried on. It ought, for instance, to make theological discussions of the person of Jesus and the resurrection less 'anxious' about logical precision, clarity, and definiteness. This is not a call for fuzzy or sentimental thinking (or for saying nothing about difficult matters); on the contrary, to take metaphorical thinking seriously is a demand for precision and clarity, though not of the logical sort. As we have seen, metaphor is the poet's way to try and define something for which there is no dictionary meaning; it is his or her

---

* 'The creed, and the "dogmatic theology" developed from it, never lose ... the character of poetry. To do so would be to lose the dramatic form of expression, and with it the expression of *living* experience and reality. To lose the *vis poetica* is at the same time to lose the *vis religiosa*. It follows, therefore, that even theology – that part of religion which treats systematically of the Deity, his nature and attributes – retains this character. ...To the question, then, whether the language of theology is also poetic language we can only answer in the following way; theological language, like metaphysical language with which it is necessarily connected, contains elements which are not poetic, but its basal elements still remain dramatic; otherwise theology would lose its touch with religion' (W. M. Urban, *Language and Reality: The Philosophy of Language and the Principles of Symbolism* [New York: Macmillan, 1939], pp. 575–576).

attempt to be precise and clear about something for which ordinary language has no way of talking. The poet mounts many metaphors, many ways of seeing 'this' as 'that,' many attempts to 'say' what cannot be said directly. The poet sets one metaphor against another and hopes that the sparks set off by the juxtaposition will ignite something in the mind as well. Hopkins' poem 'Pied Beauty' has to do with 'creation.'

> Glory be to God for dappled things –
>   For skies of couple-colour as a brinded cow;
> For rose-moles all in stipple upon trout that swim;
> Fresh-firecoal chestnut-falls; finches' wings;
>   Landscape plotted and pieced – fold, fallow, and plough;
> And all trades, their gear and tackle and trim.
> All things counter, original, spare, strange;
>   Whatever is fickle, freckled (who knows how?)
> With swift, slow; sweet, sour; adazzle, dim;
>   He fathers-forth whose beauty is past change: Praise Him.[13]

Is this less precise, clear, or definite than Barth's several hundred pages on the doctrine of creation? It is surely a different sort of precision, but, I would suggest, a more basic sort than Barth's, for Barth's vocabulary and themes rest on similarly primal, metaphorical thinking, notably biblical sources.

Moreover, if metaphor and symbol are, as Paul Ricoeur says, 'food for thought,' then they really ought to be utilized in just that way – not manipulated, translated, reduced, but contemplated, probed, reflected upon.* Ricoeur devotes an entire four hundred-page book to probing and contemplating the symbolism of evil, starting with its most primitive and physical manifestation, 'stain,' and moving carefully and thoroughly *through* the metaphors that stain is associated with – defilement, sin, guilt, bondage – to more general philosophical statements.[14] This impressive study does not translate the metaphors into terms supposedly more palatable to the

---

* Ricoeur's understanding of symbol is practically identical with my view of metaphor – in both cases there is no way *around* the image. '. . . symbolic signs are opaque, because the first, literal, obvious meaning itself points analogically to a second meaning which is not given otherwise than in it' (*The Symbolism of Evil*, trans. Emerson Buchanan [Boston: Beacon Press, 1969], p. 15).

contemporary mind but plays the metaphors off, one against the other; the reader, when finished with the book, has been led to a fuller understanding of evil, not by being *told* what evil is but through being *shown* its many faces. The process is, of course, not unlike the way in which the biblical writers deal, less systematically to be sure, with the notion of the kingdom of God. We are never given a theology of the kingdom (though theologies of the kingdom have been abstracted from the New Testament), but we are told stories about it, about people who want the kingdom and why they want it; we are shown metaphors – pearls, seeds, camels and needles, children, hungry and thirsty strangers, maidens and a bridegroom, and so on – which image it forth.

The point is that difficult, strange, unfamiliar matters must be approached with the utmost cunning, imagination, and indirection in order for them to be seen *at all*. It is one of the unfortunate assumptions that metaphor and myth belong to the childhood of the human race, or at best are mere embellishments of truth we can have, now that we are logically and technically advanced, in some more direct way, whether philosophically, scientifically, or existentially. But if new meaning is always metaphorical, then *there is no way now or ever to have strange truth directly*. We are always children, primitives, when it comes to new insight into such matters as love, life, death, God, hope, and faith. The point is, of course, that apart from metaphor, that is, apart from primal language, we would not 'see' such matters at all but would be like the rest of creation – dumb and univocal, knowing but one reference for each sign. We would simply *stay* where we are with what we are; metaphor is our unique power of movement, for we alone in creation are not locked into our 'place,' but can move from our place to a new place. Metaphor is, I believe, the heart of the matter for theological reflection, since the task of theology is to serve the hearing of God's word, that strange truth that disrupts our ordinary world and moves us – and it – to a new place.

3

Metaphor:
The Heart of the Matter

Metaphor is not first of all the language of poets but ordinary language. We use metaphors all the time in order to say something about things we know little about.* A child looking at a mountain stripped of foliage might say, 'That mountain is bald,' transferring her perception of her grandfather's pate to the mountain. I. A. Richards says, 'in the simplest formulation, when we use a metaphor we have two thoughts of different things active together and supported by a single word, or phrase, whose meaning is a resultant of their interaction.'[1] What happens in this interaction, as Max Black says, is that we use the conventional wisdom associated with one context to serve as the screen or grid through which we see the other context.

Suppose I look at the night sky through a piece of heavily smoked glass on which certain lines have been left clear. Then I shall see only the stars that can be made to lie on the lines previously prepared upon the screen, and the stars I do see will be seen as

* M. H. Abrams in *The Mirror and the Lamp* gives an excellent description of this point. 'Any area for investigation, so long as it lacks prior concepts to give it structure and an express terminology with which it can be managed, appears to the inquiring mind inchoate – either a blank, or an elusive and tantalizing confusion. Our usual recourse is, more or less deliberately, to cast about for objects which offer parallels to dimly sensed aspects of the new situation, to use the better known to elucidate the less known, to discuss the intangible in terms of the tangible. This analogical procedure seems characteristic of much intellectual enterprise. There is a good deal of wisdom in the popular locution for "what is its nature?" namely: "What's it *like?*" We tend to describe the nature of something in similes and metaphors, and the vehicles of these recurrent figures, when analyzed, often turn out to be the attributes of an implicit analogue through which we are viewing the object we describe' [London: Oxford University Press, 1953], pp. 31–32).

organized by the screen's structure. We can think of a metaphor as such a screen and the system of 'associated commonplaces' of the focal word as the network of lines upon the screen. We can say that the principal subject is 'seen through' the metaphorical expression – or, if we prefer, that the principal subject is 'projected upon' the field of the subsidiary subject.[2]

Thus, for instance, when we call God 'father' we use the commonplaces associated with fatherhood as the 'smoked glass' through which we perceive God. That metaphor is emotionally charged is obvious – the feelings we have about fatherhood influence our consequent feelings about God and vice versa. Or, to use a more mundane example, the objection that policemen have to being called 'pigs' is derived from the feelings most people have about the commonplaces associated with pigs.

But metaphors are not only emotional; they are also cognitive, and here the issue is more complex. What, in fact, do we learn about the 'principal subject' through metaphors? On the face of it, we seem to learn a good deal. To say God is 'father' appears to be a direct assertion with no qualifications. Actually, however, what we *know* is the conventional wisdom associated with the subsidiary subject – we know about fatherhood and about God only through the screen of fatherhood, or as Black says, 'the principal subject is "projected upon" the field of the subsidiary subject.' From this point of view, metaphor belongs more in the realm of faith and hope than in the realm of knowledge. Ian Ramsay says that a metaphor arises in a 'moment of insight'; thus in the parable of the Prodigal Son there must be something about the universe and our experience in it which matches the behavior of a loving father.[3] But all that we *know* prior to the metaphor is, at most, inchoate and confused; and it is *only* in and through the metaphor that we can speak of it at all. This is a crucial point, for it means that metaphorical 'knowledge' is a highly risky, uncertain, and open-ended enterprise – a maneuver of desperation, if you will – in spite of the straightforward grammatical structure of a metaphorical statement. The risk and open-endedness means that many metaphors are necessary, metaphors which will support, balance, and illuminate each other. Thus, if one calls God father, presumably one could also use the metaphors sister, brother, or mother though not jailer, sorcerer, or murderer. The associated commonplaces of the first three fit together, but they do not fit with the conventional wisdom attached to the latter set of metaphors. Of course, irony and inclusiveness are also necessary in metaphorical assertion; the metaphors of lion and lover are both used for God in the Old Testament – sentimentality is not the signature of an authentic metaphorical pattern.

Although metaphor is uncertain and risky, it is not expendable; one must live with the open-endedness since there is no way to get at the principal subject directly.* In fact, and this is central for religious metaphors, there is what one might call a shift in principal and subsidiary subjects when dealing with what is radically unfamiliar to us. For instance, when the two contexts of a metaphorical interaction are both known to us reasonably well (baldness and mountain, policemen and pigs), we are less dependent on the screen or subsidiary subject than we are when dealing with father and God. Whatever may be the prior insight about God which encourages us to use one metaphor rather than another, it is more accurate, if we attend closely to poetic and religious metaphors, to speak of the simultaneity of the moment of insight and the choice of metaphor – they appear to come together and be forever wedded. This means that our focus must be upon the metaphor in all its detail; it is as if the principal subject must become the subsidiary one, or as if the other dimension, the unknown one, were available to us *only* in and through the familiar dimension. In a religious metaphor, as we shall see in the parables, the two subjects, ordinary life and the transcendent, are so intertwined that there is no way of separating them out and, in fact, what we learn is not primarily something about God but a new way to live ordinary life. In the parables a new context, the context provided by God, is suggested for perceiving ordinary life and *this* becomes our principal focus, with knowledge about God only available to us in the form of what Michael Polanyi calls 'subsidiary awareness.' Or to say it in a slightly different way, to call a parable a metaphor does not mean that it 'points to' an unknown God, but that the world of the parable itself includes both

---

* 'We can comment *upon* the metaphor, but the metaphor itself neither needs nor invites explanation and paraphrase. Metaphorical thought is a distinctive mode of achieving insight, not to be construed as an ornamental substitute for plain thought' (Black, *Models and Metaphors*, p. 237).

the ordinary and the transcendent in a complex interaction in which each illumines the other. The order of perception in a parable is such that it keeps our eyes on our world and that world as transformed by God, not on 'God in himself.'

These introductory remarks about metaphor need now to be explained more systematically and precisely. In the following passages there are at least three levels of concern with metaphor: metaphor as the creation of new meaning – poetic metaphor; metaphor as constitutive of language – radical metaphor; metaphor as the method of all human knowledge, whether social, political, intellectual, scientific, or personal – metaphor as human movement.

. . . language is ultimately traceable to metaphor. . . .[4]

The primary Imagination I hold to be the living power and prime agent of all human perception, and as a repetition in the finite mind of the eternal act of creation in the infinite I AM.[5]

. . . no matter how widely the contents of myth and language may differ, yet the same form of mental conception is operative in both. It is the form which one may denote as *metaphorical thinking*; the nature and meaning of metaphor is what we must start with if we want to find, on the one hand, the unity of the verbal and the mythical worlds and, on the other, their differences.[6]

Now it has been pointed out by others before this that there is no other way by which real knowledge of Nature can spread and increase – by which the consciousness of humanity can actually be enlarged, and knowledge, which is at present new and private, made public, but some form of metaphor.[7]

Metaphor is as ultimate as speech itself and speech as ultimate as thought.[8]

The poetic image is the human mind claiming kinship with everything that lives or has lived, and making good its claim. In doing so, it also establishes through every metaphor an affinity between external objects.[9]

Human thought is not merely metaphoric in operation. Itself forms one term of a metaphor. The other term may consist of the cosmic universe, or any detail within it, or may reach out beyond this, in exploration. . . .This method [the poetic] calls in consciously the whole figure of the human organism of mind and body, fuses it with its own instrument of language, and from this builds up its thought in an organic and human frame by which the human being and his universe are to be related and interpreted. This is what I have been calling the human metaphor.[10]

A pastiche of this sort does little more than overwhelm with its insistence that the symbolic-metaphorical ability of the human mind is crucial to its very constitution – 'metaphor is as ultimate . . . as thought.'* No more radical suggestion of the importance of metaphor is possible, and it removes us light years from metaphor as adornment or illustration of some *known* fact or truth or feeling. The suggestion being made in all these passages is that there would be *no* known fact or truth or feeling without metaphor.

Poetic Metaphor

The easiest way to grasp metaphor is by means of the examples closest at hand – poetic metaphors; for while we could call these 'second-level' metaphors in contrast to the radical images that constitute all language, they are on a continuum with them and function in the same way. On this level there is nothing mysterious about metaphor. As Robert Frost says, 'Poetry provides the one permiss-

---

* Others say it a little differently, but with the same focus. 'Metaphor is, in essence, a very simple device: it is, quite literally, a figure of speech by which a sense or meaning that is usually associated with one sort of thing (object, or situation or occasion) is "brought over" and attached to another sort of thing' (Iredell Jenkins, *Art and the Human Enterprise* [Cambridge: Harvard University Press, 1958], p. 248); 'The poetic metaphor is "a powerful image, new for the mind, [produced] by bringing together without comparison two distant realities whose relationships (*rapports*) have been grasped by the mind alone" (Paul Reverdy). A poetic metaphor is "the use of material images to suggest immaterial relationships" (Ernest Fenellosa)' (Stanley Burnshaw, *The Seamless Web* [New York: George Braziller, 1970], p. 88); 'Metaphor is the synthesis of several units of observation into one commanding image; it is the expression of a complex idea, not by analysis, nor by direct statement, but by a sudden perception of an objective relation (Herbert Read)' (Philip Wheelwright, *The Burning Fountain: A Study in the Language of Symbolism* [Bloomington: Indiana University Press, 1968], p. 94).

ible way of saying one thing and meaning another.' G. M. Hopkins'
poem 'Heaven-Haven: A nun takes the veil' is an excellent illustration of poetic metaphor, 'of saying one thing and meaning another.'

> I have desired to go
>> Where springs not fail,
> To fields where flies no sharp and sided hail
>> And a few lilies blow.
>
> And I have asked to be
>> Where no storms come,
> Where the green swell is in the havens dumb,
>> And out of the swing of the sea.[11]

The entire poem is an extended metaphor, a familiar, sensuous
rendering of an unfamiliar and nonsensuous reality. The extraordinary power of the extended metaphor derives from the fact that the
poet keeps attention focused on the particularities of storms and
seasons while all the time referring beyond them to other things.
But within the poem are also a multitude of discrete metaphors –
'sided hail,' 'green swell,' 'havens dumb,' 'swing of the sea' – which
complicate, intensify, and comment on the larger metaphor. Aris-
totle, as often, said it quite well: 'a good metaphor implies an intuitive perception of the similarities in dissimilars.' In Hopkins' poem
the whole complex of 'a nun taking the veil' is seen as similar to
the other complex of seasonal and natural phenomena; a dialectic
between the familiar, the seasons and storms at sea, and the
unfamiliar, 'taking the veil,' is set up in which each renews and
deepens the meaning of the other. The metaphoric dialectic is a
complex one: on the one hand, the familiar and sensuous is used to
evoke the unfamiliar, and, on the other hand, the unfamiliar context
or frame in which the familiar is set allows us to see the ordinary
in a new way. That is to say, the nature imagery evokes 'taking the
veil,' *and* that strange event serves as the frame for nature, causing
us to see it now in a new light. Metaphoric insight never takes us
'out of ourselves,' but it returns us to ourselves with new insight;
it is not a mystical, static, intellectual vision, but an insight into
how ordinary human life and events can be made to move beyond
themselves by connecting them to this and to that.

Because of this dialectic of the ordinary and the strange in poetic metaphor, in which each evokes and provides the context for the other, there is no way to have the new meaning apart from the metaphor itself. Any attempt to paraphrase a metaphor immediately reveals one of the primary characteristics of a good poetic metaphor: its inseparability from 'what is being said.' A critic, when asked what a metaphor 'means,' is finally reduced to repeating the line of poetry or even the entire poem, for there is no other way of saying what is being said except in the words that were chosen to say it. Poetic metaphor is used not as an embellishment of what can be said some other way, but precisely because what is being said is new and cannot be said any other way. Take, for example, the Paolo and Francesca scene from Dante's *Divine Comedy* (Canto 5, ll. 46–50):

And as the cranes go chanting their lays, making of themselves a long line in the air, so I saw approach with long-drawn wailings shades borne on these battling winds.

This is technically a simile, not a metaphor, for it has the 'as . . . so' construction, but that is really incidental, because metaphorical power is present. The cranes and the shades of Paolo and Francesca become one, so that the feeling and insight conveyed in the passage is an amalgam of the eerie, lonely cries of the serene long lines of cranes and the wailings of the lost lovers riding 'the battling winds.' There is no embellishment or adornment here; the knowing that takes place is inseparable from the images used and is conveyed *only through them*. Cranes and dead lovers are mutually illuminated and there is no way to extricate out a meaning; the meaning is held in solution in the metaphor.

The main point in this look at poetic metaphor is that metaphor creates the new, it does not embellish the old, and it accomplishes this through seeing similarity in dissimilars. This process, in essence, is the poet's genius – the combining of old words in new ways to create new meanings. The power of metaphor is in Donne's plea to God that he 'never shall be free, / Nor ever chaste, except you ravish me,' and in Richard Wilbur's 'Beasts of my soul who long to drink / Of pure mirage,' and in Denise Levertov's 'and as you read / the sea is turning its dark pages, / turning / its dark pages.'

Radical Metaphor

To speak about metaphor as radical, however, is to say more than
that metaphor is necessary for the creation of new meaning. It is to
go beyond, or better, behind, poetic metaphor; it is to assert that
language, ordinary language, and not only the language of poets, is
metaphorical. In fact, what poets do is to take our literal words, our
dead metaphors, and by combining them in new ways, make them
capable of expressing new insight. Language, all language, is ultimately traceable to metaphor – it is the foundation of language and
thus of thought.*

To insist on the radical relation between metaphor and thought
means, then, that it is not only in poetry that the metaphor *is* the thing,
but that *all* thought is metaphorical. Of course most of our language
is not obviously metaphorical; we are surrounded by dead metaphors
which make up our literal, everyday language and which allow us to
write dictionaries. But these dead metaphors were once alive; there
appears to be no way to trace language back to some primitive time
when 'word' and 'thing' were in direct correspondence. What poets
do now, primitive people did once upon a time – both must use 'this'
for 'that,' both must approach the 'thing' elliptically and indirectly,
noting the similarities between dissimilars with no final satisfaction
of having found the one and only way to the 'thing.' Thus many
metaphors are necessary, many forays must be made to track the
prey, for, apart from mystic intuition (which itself can only be
expressed metaphorically), we have no *one* way to a thing.

If metaphor were only a poetic device we might assume that some
other means of expression, some nonpoetic language, such as ordinary
or scientific language, could give us direct access. But if all thought is
metaphorical, then we must acknowledge the open-endedness, the

* To say that metaphor is constitutive of language does not of course imply any
theory about the origin of language, a question which lies beyond the ken of science
or speculation. 'Somehow in the long temporal mystery of evolution there emerged
the power and disposition to let something – whether a body, an image, a sound, or
later a written word – stand as surrogate for something else. Therein man became
– and neither anthropologist nor philosopher can say when or how – a linguistic
animal' (Philip Wheelwright, *Metaphor and Reality* [Bloomington: Indiana University
Press, 1962], p. 19).

risk, and the tentativeness of all our interpretations.* This means that we cannot say our metaphors 'correspond' to 'what is'; at best, we can only say that they seem appropriate to our experience, they 'fit' or seem 'right.'† That such a situation is one of dis-ease is obvious, and it is tempting to try to escape such uncertainty through either literalism or subjectivity. But if metaphor is at the root of language and thought, then there is no escape. And this means, of course, no escape for religious and theological language and thought as well.

But what, more precisely, does it mean to speak of metaphor as

* David Burrell's thesis of 'the dramatic character of language' provides further substantiation for the radical character of metaphor. Ordinary language *is* metaphorical through and through, he says. There is no 'meta-level inquiry' which will unravel the ambiguous and tentative character of all our interpretations of reality. In tracing the history of analogical discourse from Plato to modern times, he asserts that whereas the Renaissance view of metaphor as decorative presumes a univocal relation between language and reality, the contemporary view – witnessed to by literary critics and language analysts, notably Wittgenstein – insists on the 'inherent theory of metaphor' which presumes no privileged set of terms in our forays on reality that are exempt from criticism and reflective discrimination. 'No metaphor can claim to be the right one because this very claim would render all others superfluous and merely decorative. Yet within limits we can recognize certain "sort-crossings" as more appropriate – at least to a given context – than others. Again within limits this kind of appropriateness can be argued for and so gradually learned. But what cannot be acquired and must be presupposed is the original reflective and critical ability which issues in *recognitions* like these: that a metaphor fits the occasion' (*Analogy and Philosophical Language* [New Haven: Yale University Press, 1973), pp. 259–260).

† The ability to discriminate and to recognize appropriate metaphors is complex. It appears to be, at least in part, an intrinsic quality, like the ability to judge a work of art as 'good.' On the face of it, there may appear to be no way to learn it. Ian Ramsay says, 'The theological model works more like the fitting of a boot or a shoe than like the "yes" or "no" of a rollcall' (*Models and Mystery* [London: Oxford University Press, 1964], p. 17). Frederick Ferré suggests a more pragmatic basis for discrimination: 'The best language at his [the religious believer's] disposal in which to formulate his ultimate beliefs may be recognized as literally false, but he has reasons to believe that his concepts are not mere falsehoods. They illuminate his experience; they organize his understanding of the world in an effective and fruitful way; they replace blank opaqueness with the elusive gleam, at least, of intelligibility. In a word, his religious images "work" for him, if his is a relatively reliable set of religious beliefs; they work, if they do work, to the furtherance of understanding, the increase of integrity and coherence in the believer's total self, and thus to the fulfillment of both thought and life' ('Metaphors, Models, and Religion,' p. 344). But in learning to discriminate among religious metaphors, participation in the religious community seems essential, for in part, at least, what the 'tradition' and 'orthodoxy' are is the recognition by many believers over many centuries of metaphors that fit and are appropriate. On this reading, 'heresy' can be seen as constituted by discarded metaphors which were tried by the church and found to be inappropriate.

the root of thought and language? It means, among other things, that the human mind, as Kant insists, *constructs* its world. Coleridge also insists on the constructive character of the mind in relation to reality, isolating the imagination as the key component in that construction. Ernst Cassirer takes both Kant's and Coleridge's categories, discursive thought and the imagination, as central. The imaginative or metaphoric form of interpreting reality is the older of the two, Cassirer claims, for primitive conceptual forms show that *naming* and not discursive reason is the most ancient form of language. The primitive urge is essentially hypostatic, seeking to distinguish, to emphasize, to hold the object of attention, to fix the object as a permanent focus of attention. This can be done only with a name, a symbol. The primitive mind, is, then, an imagining mind, 'the prime agent of all human perception,' as Coleridge says, 'and as a repetition in the finite mind of the eternal act of creation in the infinite I AM.' Cassirer points to the central issue – the hypostatizing, distinguishing character of language formation, the naming through noticing. The famous incident of Helen Keller at the pump, intuiting for the first time the connection between the stuff running through her fingers and the word, the hypostasis, 'water,' is an illustration of the process of outlining reality through naming. Gradually reality is outlined more precisely, richly, and complexly through such naming, and metaphor is at the heart of the process.* Reality is created through this incredibly complex process of metaphorical leaps, of seeing this as that; we use what we notice about one thing to 'name' (describe, call up, evoke, elicit) another thing where we notice something of the same, and hence for the first time we *see* it that new way.

The major fault with Cassirer's position – and it is a crucial fault – is his assumption that imagistic language, the language of myth and poetry, is a stage on the way toward conceptual language and is superseded by it. Fortunately, Cassirer is by no means alone in

---

* Strictly speaking, image rather than metaphor is the most accurate way of describing primitive language formation, for metaphor already implies some names or symbols which are distinguished and related in order to name events and objects more precisely. But a 'pure' or radically primitive situation in which distinct denotative symbols exist is somewhat arbitrary to imagine, for even the most primitive languages display the intricate interweavings of nomenclature that rely on the ability to think metaphorically, that is, to note similarities and differences.

asserting that the basis of language is symbolic and metaphoric, and others such as Owen Barfield and Paul Ricoeur would not banish metaphorical language to second-class status but rather see it as always crucial to the creation of linguistic significance.

Barfield, a British philosopher and literary critic, working independently from Cassirer in the 1920s came to a very similar point of view, though his perspective is more narrowly directed to poetry than is Cassirer's. Like Cassirer, Barfield understands the primitive situation as one in which figurative language predominated, a language in which words were *at once* concrete and abstract, material and immaterial, physical and mental, outer and inner. The multi-signification can be recognized in such a word as *pneuma*, used variously in biblical literature for breath, wind, air, and spirit. Gradually, the outer meanings are lost. 'Whatever else you have in language and its history . . . you certainly have a process by which words with a material, or outer, meaning somehow turn into words with only an immaterial, or inner, one.'[12] Many words for creative mental processes, such as 'conceive,' 'germinate,' 'seminal,' have a material base, indeed, a sexual base. The primitive had single meanings for words – he or she participated in an original unity of body and spirit – which referred without disjuncture to inner and outer realities.

> . . . all language has been, and some still is, imagery, in the sense that one meaning is apprehended transpiring through another. We look back and we find concomitant meanings (or uncontracted meanings that have since become, and are for us now, separable and concomitant); we find an inner meaning transpiring or showing in some way through the outer. Nonfigurative language, on the other hand, is a late arrival. What we call literal meanings, whether inner or outer, are never samples of meaning in its infancy; they are always meanings in their old age – end products of a historical process.[13]

The reason we *can* 'look through' one sense of a word to another – the reason words are translucent – is that the latent inner and outer references are both there. In primitive times sensible objects were not seen as isolated from thought and feeling. Barfield claims, as does Cassirer, that this original unity was not invented by the primitives, for it exists apart from any individual thinker; it is simply the nexus out of which human animals gradually extricated themselves and to which they long to return. The history of language, then, is one of gradual distancing from this unity; the single meanings of language split into contrasted pairs – the concrete and abstract, particular and general, objective and subjective – and it is the poet's burden and glory to attempt to return to this unity.

At this point Barfield introduces metaphor seriously, for it is the peculiar function of metaphorical discourse to restore conceptually the unity that the primitive sees perceptually. The poetic search for the 'objective correlative' is an attempt to unite the inner and the outer, to find the sensuous base for the inner reality. Strictly speaking, early language was not metaphorical – it did not need metaphor since all words had inner and outer meanings – but our language, petrified by use into objective and subjective references, needs it desperately if our use of language is to be revelatory of new insight. For metaphor follows, as Barfield says, quoting Shelley, 'the footsteps of nature'; just as knowledge arose originally through more and more complex 'naming,' so metaphor, the recognition of novel connections, is the path to new insight. Knowledge, Barfield suggests, is the accumulation of metaphors.

> . . . language does indeed appear historically as an endless process of metaphor transforming itself into meaning. Seeking for material in which to incarnate its last inspiration, imagination seizes on a suitable word or phrase, uses it as a metaphor, and so creates a meaning. The progress is from meaning, through inspiration to imagination, and from imagination through metaphor, to meaning; inspiration grasping the hitherto unapprehended, and imagination relating it to the already known.[14]

The complex tissue that results from this process is language, but the process is never complete, for what are significant, insightful words to one generation become a tired body of dead clichés to the next. One can imagine, for instance, how alive the language of Paul, John, and the other writers of the New Testament must have appeared to their contemporaries compared to how opaque and petrified it appears to many in our contemporary society.

The main point Barfield, like Cassirer, is making is that knowledge is the accumulation of metaphors; this assertion seems to be

substantiated phenomenologically on the basis of primitive conception. Cassirer and Barfield did their work in the 1920s, but their basic
perspective has been corroborated by more recent commentators of
various orientations – aesthetic, literary, philosophical, and anthropological. The organic, sacramental, ecological, biological perspective – the original unity of human beings with their environment
to which metaphor, now in a sophisticated and critical way, attempts
to return us – is a dominant one, evident in such thinkers as Pierre
Teilhard de Chardin, Alfred North Whitehead, and Paul Ricoeur.

Paul Ricoeur in his masterful book *The Symbolism of Evil* understands symbols as the presuppositions of philosophy – the symbol,
as he says, gives rise to thought. He sees this stance as admittedly
a 'wager'; but he bets on the world of symbols to give him 'a better
understanding of man and of the bond between the being of man
and the being of all beings,' because symbolic language is the original
language antecedent to both reflective and mythological discourse.
Like Cassirer and Barfield, Ricoeur sees symbolic language as
pointing to our original unity with being.

> Every symbol is finally a hierophany, a manifestation of the bond
> between man and the sacred. . . .Finally, then, it is as an index
> of the situation of man at the heart of being in which he moves,
> exists, and wills, that the symbol speaks to us. . . .All the symbols
> of guilt – deviation, wandering, captivity, – all the myths – chaos,
> blinding, mixture, fall, – speak of the situation of the being of
> man in the being of the world.[15]

Further back than this we cannot go – symbols and metaphors place
us at that nexus of 'man in the being of the world.' We never get
behind metaphor and symbol – they are at the root of all our language
and thought.*

* In a recent essay, Ricoeur makes the closest possible connection between metaphor
and reality: '. . . a discourse which makes use of metaphor has the extraordinary power
of redescribing reality. This is, I believe, the referential function of metaphorical
statement. . . .If this analysis is sound, we should have to say that metaphor not only
shatters the previous structures of our language, but also the previous structures of
what we call reality. When we ask whether metaphorical language reaches reality,
we presuppose that we already know what reality is. But if we assume that metaphor
redescribes reality, we must then assume that this reality as redescribed is itself novel
reality. . . .With metaphor we experience the metamorphosis of both language and

Metaphor as Human Movement

Cassirer, Barfield, and Ricoeur in one way or another are saying that metaphor follows the footsteps of nature; that is, metaphor follows the way the human mind *works*. Metaphor is not only a poetic device for the creation of new meaning, but metaphor is as ultimate as thought. It is and can be *the* source for new insight because all human discovery is by metaphor. Metaphor unites us and our world at a level below subject–object, mind–body; it is the nexus of 'man in the being of the world,' the intimation of our original unity with all that is. To see connections, to unite this with that, is the distinctive nature of human thought; only human beings, it appears, can make novel connections within their familiar worlds in order to move beyond where they are.

Metaphor is, for human beings, what instinctual groping is for the rest of the universe – the power of getting from here to there.* We use what we have, who we are, where we are to grope toward what we dimly feel, think, and envision we might have, who we might be, where we might be. We do this through a process in which the imagination is the chief mover, setting the familiar in an unfamiliar context so that new possibilities can be glimpsed. The future is never an abstraction totally unrelated to our particular and familiar presents and pasts; it is the sometimes subtle, sometimes violent renovation and fulfillment of what is familiar to us. This is such a common and at the same time complex process that often we are unaware of it, but it is the substance of the 'movement' intimated by our daydreams and our personal utopias. It is at the basis of all critical thinking, as Herbert Marcuse makes clear in his critique of one-dimensional thought, the thought that does *not* move

---

reality' ('Creativity in Language: Word, Polysemy, Metaphor,' *Philosophy Today* [Summer 1973], pp. 110, 111).
* I am deeply indebted to Elizabeth Sewell's *The Orphic Voice* (New Haven: Yale University Press, 1960) and *The Human Metaphor* (Notre Dame: University of Notre Dame Press, 1964) for the perspective ingredient in the following remarks. As she makes clear in her books, however, the notion that the human 'method' of knowing (as well as growth in all other areas, whether personal, political, or social) is metaphorical is as old as Orpheus and as modern as Michael Polanyi. The idea that human beings think like machines rather than like organisms is a fairly recent one, as she points out – as recent as Descartes at the earliest.

because it envisions no movement which can both negate and fulfill it. Two-dimensional thought criticizes 'what is' by means of 'what might be' – its negative, that which stands over against it, provides a new context for 'what is,' not in order to destroy it but to *move* beyond it. It is the basis of Christian hope, of Jesus as the parable of the kingdom; the kingdom provides the context for 'reading' the story of Jesus as a new story; a story which is the prolepsis of the kingdom.* It is the basis of scientific discovery, the intuitive flash, the overview, as Whitehead says, which surveys the terrain from the heights, eventually to return to earth to test the hypothesis.† It is the basis of social and political revolution, which relies on the dreams of the imagination to propel us from where we are to where we might be. Metaphor is movement, human movement; without it, we would not be what we are – the only creatures in the universe to our knowledge who can *envision* a future and consciously work toward achieving it. The process is a dialectic of imagining new frames and contexts for our ordinary worlds, of seeing a new world which is also the old world. Metaphorical movement insists that the dream turn toward and renovate reality, not escape from it.

Metaphorical thinking, then, is not simply poetic language nor primitive language; it is the way human beings, selves (not mere minds) *move* in all areas of discovery, whether these be scientific,

* In the perspective called 'theology of hope' (Jürgen Moltmann, Dorothee Soelle, Gustavo Gutierrez, etc.) the future functions as the context in which the present can be both criticized and renovated. The claim of these theologians that Christianity is always and basically eschatological can be accepted, provided such a perspective does not discard the present. That is, the kingdom is not only ahead of us and over against us but it is also in our midst – in the healing stories, the parables, the cross and resurrection of Jesus of Nazareth we have intimations, metaphors, of the kingdom.
† Ian G. Barbour insists that the construction of scientific models, like the construction of religious metaphors, is *the* way of perceiving and redescribing reality. 'I will deal . . . with theoretical models in science, which are mental constructs devised to account for observed phenomena in the natural world. They originate in a combination of analogy to the familiar and creative imagination in the invention of the new. I will argue that theoretical models, such as the "billiard ball model" of a gas, are not merely convenient calculating devices or temporary psychological aids in the formulation of theories; they have an important continuing role in suggesting both modifications in existing theories and the discovery of new phenomena. I will try to show that such models are taken seriously but not literally. They are neither literal pictures of reality nor "useful fictions," but partial and provisional ways of imagining what is not observable; they are symbolic representation of aspects of the world which are not directly accessible to us' (*Myths, Models and Paradigms*, pp. 6–7).

religious, poetic, social, political, or personal. The old Cartesian dichotomy between mind and body, objective and subjective, thought and feeling is not relevant to a radically metaphorical pattern of human movement and growth; human beings are organisms, not machines, and like other organisms they 'grope,' but in a special way, a conscious way, which means that their special 'thing' is their ability to make novel connections and associations within their familiar environment, dislocating it sufficiently so that the old, the stale, the ordinary, 'what is,' is seen in a new light as what might be.

The base of such movement is undoubtedly erotic – the desire, as Coleridge and Ricoeur have intimated, to be united with 'what is.' It is the desire for fulfillment, for ultimate consummation, of one's entire being. Plato's myth of human thought in the image of the search for the androgynous human being is dead center and radically metaphorical, for if one understands the method of human thought as metaphorical, it *is* more like sexual union than it is like 'thinking.' Or as Elizabeth Sewell says, 'Human thought is not merely metaphoric in operation. Itself forms one term of the metaphor. The other may consist of the cosmic universe, or any detail within it, or may reach out beyond this, in exploration.'[16] Human beings, says Sewell, take themselves, their bodies, and where those bodies are and what they are, in all their particularity and concreteness and richness, as the 'figure,' the image, in terms of which they 'understand,' learn about, fathom *whatever* it is they are concerned to fathom. The unknown lies all about us and we 'figure' it all with ourselves – the human metaphors. Our movement, of whatever sort, is always metaphorical, with ourselves as one term of the metaphor.

What is at stake in this perspective is epistemologically radical; that is, it is *not* being proposed that metaphorical language simply 'has a place' in human knowing, a place ultimately superseded by conceptual language, as Cassirer would maintain. Rather metaphor, as Sewell understands it, is *the human method of investigating the universe*.* And if the problem of human knowing, as one commen-

---

* An epistemological extreme of Sewell's position of the human being as the metaphor or partner in all knowing is James Olney's *Metaphors of the Self: The Meaning of Autobiography*: 'A theology, a philosophy, a physics or a metaphysics – properly seen, these are all autobiography recorded in other characters and other symbols. . . . A metaphor . . . through which we stamp our own image on the face of nature, allows

tator on Sewell has written, is 'How does one investigate, interpret, inquire into a system of which the observer is an inseparable part?' then the answer must *include* the observer at every point; it must be a method in which 'one figures itself in on whatever figuring process one is at work upon.'[17] The main difficulty with post-Cartesian epistemologies is that they do not figure in the figurer; they split mind and body, reason and imagination, subject and object, nature and history and end with something other and less than *human* knowing.

The banishment of imprecise, metaphorical language from the realm of serious reflection and discourse entailed the eventual loss of poetry as a unique and useful *method* of inquiry, however enjoyable and even important it was to remain as aesthetically interesting *subject matter*. Poetry, with its roots reaching far below the surface dualisms of reason/imagination, mind/matter, nature/history, had relied upon the unity of man's sensibility coextensive with the movements of nature as expressed primordially and paradigmatically in the figure of man's own body as embodying its own inescapable method of knowing the living universe; early Greek philosophy, founded as it was upon the denial of these roots, sought to provide man with a myth of himself and the world which itself precluded man's mythmaking capacity and thereby so exteriorized and fragmented man's own conception of himself that the forms upon which he had earlier relied as paradigmatic for expressing his self-conception were necessarily discredited Being quite literally 'uprooted,' the mental side of man's meaning-giving powers relinquished its understanding of itself as inevitably conjoined with the body's own form and with the world as possible clues to the way man 'figures' his own understanding.[18]

An analysis such as the above indicates that the importance of metaphor can scarcely be overstated. Its claim is that *human* knowing,

us to connect the known of ourselves to the unknown of the world, and, making available new relational patterns, it simultaneously organizes the self into a new and richer entity; so that the old known self is joined to and transformed into the new, the heretofore unknown, self. Metaphor says very little about what the world is, or is like, but a great deal about what I am . . .' ([Princeton: Princeton University Press, 1972], pp. 5, 31–32).

at its most profound, is not disembodied, abstract, or conceptual; the analogy for human knowing is not the Cartesian machine but the evolutionary organism – the stretching of the whole creature beyond itself into the unknown. With the rest of the universe this 'groping' toward richer and more fruitful forms is unconscious, with the human being it is conscious; but the pattern is the same. Nothing is left behind, no matter is sloughed off. Metaphor is the language of 'a body that thinks'; it is, therefore, neither an embellishment of language nor a primitive form to be superseded by conceptual language, but *the* method of human thought.

A superb example of metaphor as the method of human thought is Walter Ong's analysis of the death of one of the five nuns in Gerard Manley Hopkins' poem 'The Wreck of the Deutschland.' Hopkins' treatment of the nun's death and her constant cry, 'O Christ, come quickly,' is movement through figuring with the whole self.

> This was the point – unknown until now – to which her life had been building up, and she was ready, for she had known that God's coming need not be gentle, that He is present not only in 'the stars, lovely-asunder' or in 'the dapple-with-damson west,' but in all events of history, even the most horrible, out of which He can bring joy. . . .[Hopkins'] fascination with the unique and his sense of historicity is shown perhaps most strikingly by the way in which in the 'Deutschland' he has fixed on the consciously accepted death of a human being – the utterly unique culmination of an utterly unique existence – as the very focus of existence and meaning.[19]

All the ingredients of the human metaphor are here in a most extreme form in this human life at its moment of death. The nun sees her *own death*, the culmination of all she has become, as the means, the method, for moving to where she would be – with Christ. It is absurd to think of concepts of grace or life or death; one can only say that *she*, her whole life now at its culmination, is the metaphor which alone is at her disposal to use to go beyond where she now is, at the entrance to death. What is true of the culmination of life in death is true also of its passage – movement is by the human metaphor, the entire self in its embodied, historical, individual reality.

If human beings move like this in all ways in which they do move, and if this movement is not merely off the top of the head but is a total movement of the total self, then metaphor, grounded as it is in the sensuous stuff of the earth and the body and the familiar, is not only the method, but metaphors are the appropriate expression of the method. For metaphorical language not only connects this with that, here with there, but demands that one partner of the association, at least, be concrete, sensuous, familiar, bodily. It will abide no abstractions, no head without a body, no mystical flights, but because it is the method of *human* movement it insists on taking along the whole human being in all its familiarity, messiness, and concreteness. This means, among other things, that 'anthropomorphic' language (metaphoric language) is, as Sewell says, what human language is bound to be; and she adds, What else could it be? Human beings cannot think (or move) in nonhuman ways: given what we are, we must think and move 'anthropomorphically.'[20]

Much of this seems so self-evident that we wonder why we miss it so often; why we insist on trying to step out of our skins when we think. Theological thinking has often been prone to this attempt in spite of the fact that it is so patently opposed by the universally accepted belief (however interpreted) that God is somehow with us in the *human* life and death of Jesus of Nazareth, and opposed as well by the anthropomorphic, metaphorical language of the Scriptures, not to mention the highly 'existential' genres in which the Scriptures are written – the passion story, hymns, letters, sermons, poetry, and so on. As we have already noted, Erich Auerbach has pointed out in several of his writings that it was Christianity and particularly the story of Jesus that gave to Western letters and thought its trust in the human, its sense of the importance of human life, and its hope that it might get somewhere. The metaphorical tradition – the willingness to trust the familiar sufficiently to use it as one partner in the associations to move beyond it – is in large part the legacy of Christianity, yet the main tradition in Christian theology has often retreated from faith in its own foundation.

Metaphor, as we have described it, is *the* way of human knowing. It is not simply a way of embellishing something we can know in some other way. There is no other way. If this is so, then human knowledge (of whatever sort) has certain characteristics: it is tenta-

tive, relativistic, multi-layered, dynamic, complex, sensuous, historical, and participatory. But the language of theology, for instance,
often seems not to have these characteristics. It often appears to fall
into what Philip Wheelwright calls 'steno-language,' what Barfield
calls rational language, what Cassirer calls scientific language.

We have seen that modern languages are for the most part
composed of dead metaphors; common sense or discursive language
was once metaphorical but now has attained a univocal meaning.
Discursive language, then, the language which relates, communicates, designates, measures, enumerates, dissects, analyzes, systematizes, depends on metaphorical language – it is, in fact, the old
age of such language. The rational deals with what is delivered to
it; it analyzes, dissects, systematizes the fruit of the imagination –
symbolic, mythological, metaphorical language; discursive language
rearranges the already known. It would be wrong, of course, to
understand this division in such a way as to suppose that poetry is
without logical language and philosophy and science without metaphorical language, for, from scientists and from scientifically-based
philosophers such as Polanyi, Whitehead, and Teilhard we know
that the intuitive leaps of creative scientists are very similar to the
metaphoric process; and no one has ever claimed that Dante or
Shakespeare did not think logically. The relations between the two
types of language are highly complex, symbiotic, and impure. Moreover, aesthetic experience is precisely 'the *felt* change of consciousness' (Barfield) from prosaic language to poetic, and if it were not
for prosaic language to hold a world in order, the awareness of *new*
connections would not be possible.

It is true that abstract thought and language is the latest and
therefore some have said it is the highest human accomplishment.
There is certainly a progression of language toward the abstract; it
appears to be the natural completion of symbolic language. But it
is an unfortunate development, particularly as we shall see in theology, to consider the natural completion of language as its 'highest'
development. For it has meant, in large measure, the hegemony of
abstract, systematic language in theological reflection, the elevation
of the great systematizers – Thomas Aquinas, Calvin, Schleiermacher, Tillich, Barth – and the accompanying depression of more
basic forms, such primary forms of religious reflection as parable,
story, poem, and confession. It is upon these primary forms – meta-

phorical forms – that all theological reflection relies. As Robert Funk says, the parable lies somewhere behind systematic theology: how the parable informs theology is the heart of our concern.* But a few guidelines for what I have called intermediary theology may be emerging:

1) the various forms of metaphorical language operative in biblical literature and in the Christian literary tradition ought to be looked at carefully as resources for theological reflection;

2) these forms are not secondary embellishments to the mainline systematic and doctrinal tradition, but are, in fact, its nourishment;

3) recognizing the importance of such forms as parable, story, poem, and confession does not imply substituting these forms for systematic theology, but it does imply a continuum from these forms to systematic theology.

These guidelines (or some like them) are not choices made arbitrarily. If one accepts the thesis of this chapter that metaphor is basic not only to new meaning (poetic metaphor) and to the formation of language (radical metaphor) but to all human thought of whatever sort – if, to put it most sharply, all our theories, revolutions, dreams, works of art, scientific discoveries, and metaphysics, not to mention our personal lives, are attempts to 'figure' the universe – then there is no way for theological reflection to avoid a return to its metaphorical base in parable, story, poem, and confession. It is imperative that we now look carefully at one of these metaphorical forms – the parable – before attempting to say more about intermediary theology.

---

* Paul Ricoeur makes some interesting comments on parables and systematic theology in an essay entitled 'Listening to the Parables of Jesus' (*Criterion*, 13 [Spring 1974], 18–22). He contends that Jesus' parables are 'a language which from beginning to end, *thinks through* the Metaphor and never *beyond*.' We who are used to using images as provisional devices to be replaced by concepts find the strategy of the parables hard to bear, but, says Ricoeur, our disappointment at not finding 'a coherent idea, an equivocal concept from this bundle of metaphors' can become amazement when we realize that 'there is more in the Parables taken together than in any conceptual system about God. We are, in the Parables taken as a whole, given much more to *think through* than the coherence of any concept offers.' We can, he says, 'draw from the Parables nearly all the kinds of theologies which have divided Christianity through the centuries . . . and taken all together, they say more than any rational theology.' The parables, in words Ricoeur has used elsewhere, 'give rise to thought,' but cannot be reduced to 'theological simplifications which we attempt to put in their place.'

4

The Parable:
The Primary Form

It was very early in the morning, the streets clean and deserted, I was on my way to the railroad station. As I compared the tower clock with my watch I realized it was already much later than I had thought, I had to hurry, the shock of this discovery made me feel uncertain of my way, I was not very well acquainted with the town as yet, fortunately there was a policeman nearby, I ran to him and breathlessly asked him the way. He smiled and said: 'From me you want to learn the way?' 'Yes,' I said, 'since I cannot find it myself.' 'Give it up, give it up,' said he, and turned away with a great sweep, like someone who wants to be alone with his laughter.[1]

This parable by Franz Kafka seems, on a first reading, to invite interpretation – in fact, to insist on it. One can immediately think of autobiographical, psychological, and theological interpretations which might 'make sense' out of it. But to attempt such interpretations would be to allegorize it, to treat it as an illustration or embellishment of what we 'already know.' And all the interpretations do, in fact, fall flat; they are far less interesting than the story itself, and even though they may comfort us for a while with the supposition that we now understand the parable, we find ourselves returning again and again to the story, unsatisfied with *any* interpretation. The parable appears to be more and other than any interpretation.

This is so, I believe, because Kafka's parable is a genuine one – it is not translatable or reducible. It is also an excellent parable to ponder because, if anything, it is even less 'translatable' than biblical parables while manifesting many of the same central qualities.

The setting is ostensibly very ordinary: someone, up early in the morning, is rushing through the streets to the railroad station. The sense of haste is heightened by the run-on phrases, punctuated mainly by commas and by the gradual build-up of the person's awareness that 'it was already much later than I had thought.' A surrealistic note is introduced when the comparison of his watch with the tower clock so shocks him that he is 'uncertain of the way.' We pause – is that comparison sufficient to make him lose his way? Our credulity is stretched, but not broken. Troubles seem to mount – the person is late, the streets deserted, he is uncertain of the way, and he is apparently new in town – but with 'fortunately' we breathe more easily and feel the story will take a turn for the better. Policemen always know their way about town and our credulity is restored completely when the stranger asks the officer 'the way' (though we note in passing that he does not add 'to the railroad station'). We are, however, unprepared for the answer and even more disturbed – even dumbfounded – by the final reply, 'Give it up.' The realism of the story has been cracked and through it we glimpse *something* – but what?

This parable is an extended metaphor, and, as a genuine metaphor, it is not translatable into concepts. To be sure, it is shot through with open-endedness, with pregnant silences, with cracks opening into mystery. But it remains profoundly impenetrable. It is, as we shall see, far more impenetrable than biblical parables because what Kafka's parables are all 'about' is simply the incomprehensibility of the incomprehensible. Kafka's parables, like all genuine parables, are themselves actuality – the parables are a figurative representation of an actual, total meaning, so they do not 'stand for' anything but *are* life. This means we must make a very careful analysis of all the parts of the parable for they *are* the *meaning* of it. The meaning is not a separate realm, something that can be pointed to; the totality of all the processes of life and thought in the parable *is* its meaning. What this totality of all the processes of life and thought amounted to in Kafka's parables was the incomprehensibility of the incomprehensible; but this is not an extrinsic meaning – it is *what the story says.*

And again Jesus spoke to them in parables saying, 'The kingdom of heaven may be compared to a king who gave a marriage feast for his son, and sent his servants to call those who were invited to the marriage feast; but they would not come. Again he sent other servants, saying, "Tell those who are invited, Behold, I have made ready my dinner, my oxen and my fat calves are killed, and everything is ready; come to the marriage feast." But they made light of it and went off, one to his farm, another to his business, while the rest seized his servants, treated them shamefully, and killed them. The king was angry, and sent his troops and destroyed those murderers and burned their city. Then he said to his servants, "The wedding is ready, but those invited were not worthy. Go therefore to the thoroughfares, and invite to the marriage feast as many as you find." And those servants went out into the streets and gathered all whom they found, both bad and good; so the wedding hall was filled with guests.'

(Matt. 22:1–10; cf. Luke 14:16–24)

Initially we may feel on much more solid ground in this parable of the Wedding Feast than with Kafka's parable.* The parable starts off as a simile rather than a metaphor and this is a relief: 'The kingdom of heaven may be compared to. . . .' But while the grammar may suggest a simile – an image that illustrates what we already know – it is obvious that we do have a genuine metaphor here, not only because we do not 'already know' what the kingdom of heaven is but also because the image put forth – the ensuing story – is not a discrete comparison but a whole nexus of images, a total situation, an extended metaphor. So we are not much better off than we were when faced with Kafka's parable, though, from an analysis of the parable *itself*, I think we will discover that what the story says is other than the incomprehensibility of the incomprehensible.

The first thing to do with a parable is to read it, several times, work out the relations of those involved, highlight the subtleties of the story – in other words, let the story penetrate *us*, rather than

---

* In the comments on this parable and to a lesser extent in the general discussion of parables that follows, I am indebted to Robert W. Funk, particularly his book *Language, Hermeneutic and Word of God*. I do not go into historical critical questions about the parables but as a layperson in the field of New Testament scholarship have relied heavily on the crucial work done on the parables by Joachim Jeremias, C. H. Dodd, A. T. Cadoux, Amos Wilder, Dan Via, and Norman Perrin. My remarks are meant not to add to that body of work but to relate their findings to my central thesis of the importance of parable to theology.

look around for possible interpretations of it. The host is the king, an important, if not *the* important man around, and he gives a marriage feast for his son – the setting is one of high import. The guest list presumably includes the 'best' people (the ones with farms, businesses, well-spread tables). The setting is realistic, and in keeping with this realism the king is inviting those on the social register to his son's wedding. The first awkward and unexpected note is introduced with 'but they would not come.' What possible excuses could *anyone* give for refusing to come to such a dinner, and why should *those* people especially want to refuse the invitation? The king, with unusual generosity and patience, we feel, persists; not only that, he describes in luscious detail the dinner – appealing not to their respect for their king or even to their common courtesy, but to their stomachs! The list of delights to be had at the feast ends with a sweeping assertion, 'everything is ready,' and with a supplication, 'come to the marriage feast.' The realism is strained and we are surprised at their responses: one group is indifferent, the other violent. The molestation and murder of the servants strikes the reader with a shock not unlike the 'Give it up' of the smiling policeman in Kafka's parable. In both instances a deep crack breaks the surface realism and we glimpse something through it; the context or frame of the story is something out of the ordinary. The king's anger, on the other hand, seems justified, and it is total – the guests are wiped out. At this point a second movement begins in the story: the invitation to others, and the invitation is as total as was the liquidation of the first guests. Once again the frame of the story is not the ordinary one. The servants go 'into the streets' and invite indiscriminately 'both bad and good' until the hall is filled.

This story is by no means incomprehensible, but neither is it a story with a 'moral' or with 'one point,' two ways of interpreting parables which many New Testament scholars have until late embraced and which many preachers still embrace. It is, first of all, as Robert Funk says, 'a paradigm of reality.' It is, however, a paradigm of reality as seen in a novel context – one in which 'everydayness' is no longer the accepted criterion. Funk speaks of two 'logics' of viewing reality in the parable with which the structure of the story and the relations of characters present us.[2] These are, of course, the logics of merit and of grace, or to put it less theologically, the logic of those who view reality in everyday terms and those who view it in a surprising, new context, the perspective of receiving what one does not deserve. The first invitations are offered to the worthy; the second invitations are proffered with no regard to worth.

This comment leads to a second point, for the insight that comes – the new 'logic' – is dependent on the deformation of the old 'logic.' We recall Owen Barfield's comment that the aesthetic moment, the moment of new insight, always involves 'a felt change of consciousness,' which occurs when everyday language is used in an unfamiliar context. Metaphorical language, parabolic language, does not take us out of everyday reality but drives us more deeply into it, deforming our usual apprehensions in such a way that we see that reality in a new way. The second 'logic' like all new meaning is a deepening of reality, not an escape from it into a never-never land. What we see, then, in the parable of the Wedding Feast is not a new reality but the same reality in a new perspective.* The mundane world is transmuted; no new world is created. In both 'logics,' the 'world' is the story of the wedding feast; what changes is the guest list – those who will accept the invitation to the feast. This is an important point, for it means that there is no two-world thinking here – a 'secular' and a 'religious' perspective; rather the question is a secular and a mundane one, the question of two specific ways of comporting oneself with reality. As genuine metaphors, parables could not do other than turn us toward reality, for, as Wallace Stevens says, the purpose of 'the symbolic language of metamorphosis' is to intensify one's sense of reality. Or, as Philip Wheelwright puts it: 'What really matters in a metaphor is the psychic depth at which the things of the world, whether actual or fancied, are transmuted by the cool heat of the imagination.'[3] If there were a 'turn' in the parable of the Wedding Feast away from the everyday, if the gracious closing invitation of the king took our attention away from the concrete story, the parable would be neither a good metaphor nor, as Gerhard Ebeling claims it to be, 'the linguistic incarnation,' the form of language most appropriate to the incarnation.[4]

This is not to say, of course, that the dimension of grace is passed

---

* 'The parable cannot be accommodated in the "logic" of everydayness, but neither can it dispense with language attuned to the mundane world; the metaphorical language brings the familiar into the unfamiliar context and distorts it, in order to call attention to it anew, i.e., to bring it into a new frame of reference, a new referential totality' (Funk, *Language*, p. 195).

over in silence in the story. The world of the parable includes *both* the secular and the religious, but with a primary focus on the secular.* In Max Black's terminology, the story is the screen or 'smoked glass' through which we perceive the new logic of grace; or as Philip Wheelwright says, assertions about this dimension are made 'lightly' or in 'soft focus'; or as Michael Polanyi would claim, our focal awareness is on the story, our subsidiary awareness on its transcendent dimensions. A New Testament parable is a 'linguistic incarnation' and, like its teller, who himself was the parable of God, works by indirection, by, as Leander Keck says, framing 'familiar elements in unfamiliar plots.'[5] The spectators must participate imaginatively, must so live in the story that insight into its strangeness and novelty come home to them. They are not *told* about the graciousness of God in a parable but are *shown* a situation of ordinary life which has been revolutionized by grace. In other words, parables, and Jesus as a parable, operate in the way metaphor does.

Finally we are brought to a third point: we do not interpret the parable, but the parable interprets us. This watchword of the new hermeneutic is neither a slogan nor a conundrum: it is simply the consequence of taking the parable as metaphor seriously. Metaphors cannot be 'interpreted' – a metaphor does not have a message; it *is* a message. If we have really focused on the parable, if we have let it work on us (rather than working on it to abstract out its 'meaning'), we find that we are interpreted.† That is, we find ourselves identifying with one of the two guest lists – our own logic toward reality is illuminated. In this parable, as in the Prodigal Son and many others (though by no means all) some hear and understand and accept the unmerited invitation and some do not.

* A parallel point in regard to the focus of the parables is made by Norman Perrin: 'It is a remarkable and little noted fact that . . . there is only a very limited number of parables which are concerned to proclaim the Kingdom of God *per se*. The vast majority of them are concerned with the experience and/or subsequent activity of men confronted by the reality of God at work' (*Rediscovering the Teaching of Jesus* [New York: Harper and Row, 1967], p. 83). It is not primarily knowing about the kingdom that appears to be crucial in the parables, but rather deciding when confronted by it. The emphasis is secular, human, and individual.

† '. . . the word of God, like a great work of art, is not on trial. The work of art exists in its own right, to be viewed and contemplated, received or dismissed, but not reconstructed. The text, too, although shaped by human hands, stands there to be read and pondered, but not manipulated . . .' (Funk, *Language*, pp. 11–12).

Parables as Metaphors

Parables have not always, or usually, been viewed as metaphors.* Historical criticism tended to focus on 'what a parable meant' in its historical context (C. H. Dodd and Joachim Jeremias). This approach is perhaps an advance over Jülicher, whose 'one-point' interpretation tended to reduce the parables to their ideational possibilities, evidencing little if any appreciation for them as metaphors, in other words, as nonreducible entities. A metaphor is neither reducible to one point nor is its 'meaning' foreclosed in some historical moment: it is rather generative of *new* meanings in the plural. C. H. Dodd's definition of Jesus' parables does point to other possibilities.

> At its simplest the parable is a metaphor or simile drawn from nature or common life, arresting the hearer by its vividness or strangeness, and leaving the mind in sufficient doubt about its precise application to tease it into active thought.[6]

The emphasis on strangeness, doubt, and teasing into active thought preclude the reduction of the parabolic form to one point or to a purely historical interpretation. Amos Wilder indicates the same direction when he conceives of the parable as a metaphor in which 'we have an image with a certain shock to the imagination which directly conveys vision of what is signified.'[7]

But before we can speak directly of the 'certain shock to the imagination' which the parable form effects, we must look at its setting – not its historical setting (a question for the New Testament scholars to debate) but its setting as an aesthetic object. As an extended metaphor, the parable is an aesthetic object – and we shall have more to say about this – but, it seems to me, an aesthetic object of a special sort. For to a greater degree than other aesthetic objects, such as an Eliot poem or a Tolstoy novel, the setting of the parable is triangular. The components of the triangle are source or author (Jesus as narrator), the aesthetic object (the parable narrated), and the effect (the listeners to whom the parable is narrated). This

* Of recent Biblical scholars, only A. T. Cadoux, Amos Wilder, Norman Perrin, Dan Via, Robert Funk, and John Dominic Crossan so view them consistently.

triangle pattern points to the original situation of the parables: *Jesus told stories to people*. All three factors should operate in any analysis of the parables, for they cannot be abstracted from their source or from their listeners. As Norman Perrin points out, there are three kinds of interpretation involved in *any* textual criticism: historical, literary, and hermeneutical; that is, criticism of *who* tells or writes, *what* is told or written, and to *whom* the text is directed.[8]

The parables present a special case, however, for the point of Jesus' parables is not mere illumination, aesthetic insight, or secret wisdom. There is a stress in the parables on confrontation and decision, an emphasis not evident in most other aesthetic objects. 'The parables of Jesus were directed to a specific situation, the situation of men and women confronted by the imminence of the irruption of God into their world.'[9] Hence, while the three components of the interpretative triangle are crucial, there is an emphasis on the third, on the listeners, though, as we shall see, the power of the confrontation occurs only because of *who* told the parables and *what* is being told to them.

The first component of the triangle, Jesus as narrator, is perhaps the most difficult. We are all well aware of the pitfalls of the Intentional Fallacy, the deleterious effects on the integrity of the aesthetic object through interpretation by means of the 'intentions' of the artist. And we have no desire to fall into that trap, not because it is unfashionable but because if we take the parable as metaphor seriously, attention must be focused on the parable itself and not on its authority or source. Two qualifications can be made, however. First, it does matter, in the instance of the biblical parables, that Jesus and not someone else told them. They are, as Perrin points out, 'highly personal texts' which express 'the vision of reality of their author,' and that vision 'cannot be contemplated except in dialogue with their creator.'[10] The 'voice' which calls us (as Walter Ong would put it) in the parables is the voice of Jesus.[11] The best way to his vision is through the parables, for, as New Testament scholars agree, the parables not only are Jesus' most characteristic form of teaching but are among the most authentic strata in the New Testament. Hence our attention should not be diverted from the parables to the intentions of their author, for it is only by giving extraordinary attention to the parables themselves that we hear that voice and understand that vision.

Second, Jesus is related to the parables obliquely, not directly. As we noted in the parable of the Wedding Feast, the attention of the listeners is directed not toward the speaker nor toward 'religious' questions, but toward two 'logics' of comporting oneself with reality. As Robert Funk points out, Jesus, as the speaker of the parable, brings the new 'logic' near and in this sense the parable can be considered as 'the self-attestation of Jesus, i.e., as the inverbalization of Jesus as the word,' but the self-attestation is hidden and indirect – 'the parable is an oblique invitation on the part of Jesus to follow him. Since Jesus belongs to the situation figured in the parable, it is he who has embarked upon this way, who lives out of the new "logic".'[12] In summary, then, it is necessary to attend in a New Testament parable to Jesus as the speaker of the parables, but this can and ought to be done in a way that not only retains their integrity as aesthetic objects but in fact pushes us to focus on the parables themselves.

A second component of the triangle, the listeners, is as essential for a just appreciation of the situation of the parables as is Jesus as narrator. In fact, extraordinary attention is being paid to the listeners by current biblical scholarship: the heart of the new hermeneutic project is, as we have seen, not the interpretation of the parables, but the interpretation of the listeners *by* the parables. To return again to the parable of the Wedding Feast, the way in which the hearers 'hear' the parable, whether they align themselves with the old 'logic' of everydayness or with the new 'logic' of grace, interprets them. They are interpreted, understood, defined by their response. And this emphasis by current scholarship on the hearers is not merely an attempt to make the parables 'relevant' to today's people; the parables in the New Testament are set in deeply controversial contexts – they are told in response to questions, accusations, demands, and are meant to involve the listeners directly as participants. Implied in parable after parable is the question, 'And what do *you* say? What will *you* do?' In fact, as we saw in the parable of the Wedding Feast, the structure of the story – its two 'logics' – is predicated on the basis of bringing the listeners, indirectly, to a decision. But again, as with Jesus the speaker, the importance of the role of the listeners does not turn our attention away from the parable but toward it. For we need not and ought not commit the Affective Fallacy at this point – interpreting the parable by means of its effect on the listeners. Rather, concern with the effect forces us back to the parable itself, for if we are to gain *new* insight, if the parable is to work its effect, there is no way to accomplish this but through maximum attention to its own givens, to the parable as metaphor.

We are brought, then, to the parable itself as the way to hear the voice it embodies and the challenge it presents to us. The two central features of the parable as aesthetic object are its realism and its strangeness. In Jesus' parable of the Wedding Feast the realistic story is primary, and this is true of all of Jesus' parables. They are about people getting married, wayward sons, widows on limited incomes, migrant workers, doctors and patients, fools and wise men, and so on. The commonness of the parables, their secularity and mundanity, has been acknowledged and appreciated by all, and it is such an obvious trait that we might be inclined to overlook its importance. But it is special when compared with other bodies of religious literature where gods and their doings (the Greeks), hierarchies of aeons and quasi-deities (the Gnostics), wise sayings and admonitions (the Buddhists) predominate. The Sermon on the Mount, a collection of Jesus' sayings and teachings, is throughout metaphorical – the teaching is evoked in terms of salt losing its savor, lamps under bushels, temple gifts versus brotherly reconciliation, plucked-out eyes and dismembered bodies, an eye for an eye, coats and cloaks, treasures eaten by moth and rust, lilies of the field, birds of the air, pearls before swine, loaves and stones, fishes and serpents. The list of New Testament metaphors seems endless and little needs to be said about the extensiveness and commonness of biblical imagery. But it does need to be stressed that it is *there* and is the *dominant* language of the New Testament.

This realism is not the same as Homeric realism – it is not mere surface detail, all in the 'foreground.' Rather it is realism 'fraught with background,' as Erich Auerbach puts it, and this 'background,' in both the Old Testament and the New, is the 'way' the Judaic-Christian tradition has handled the matter of speaking of the divine. *The only legitimate way of speaking of the incursion of the divine into history, or so it appears to this tradition, is metaphorically.* Metaphor is proper to the subject-matter because God remains hidden.[13] The belief that Jesus is the word of God – that God is manifest somehow in a human life – does not dissipate metaphor but in fact intensifies its centrality, for what is more indirect – a more complete union of the realistic and the strange – than a human life as the abode of the divine? Jesus as the word is metaphor par excellence; he is the parable of God.

It is entirely natural or inevitable, then, that the realism of the parables is of a special sort, that it provides again and again 'that certain shock to the imagination' which Amos Wilder mentions. The way this shock is conveyed initially is the assumption of the parables that important things happen and are decided at the every-day level. The parables again and again indicate that it is in the seemingly insignificant events of being invited to a party and refusing to go, being jealous of a younger brother who seems to have it all his way, resenting other workers who get the same pay for less work, that the ultimate questions of life are decided.

> The 'field' which the parable thus conjures up is not merely this or that isolated piece of earthiness, but the very tissue of reality, the nexus of relations, which constitutes the arena of human existence where life is won or lost.[14]

The 'shock,' in the first instance, consists in realizing, say in the parable of the Wedding Feast, that one's casual refusal to accept a gracious invitation apparently has something to do with whether one lives or dies. How can this be? But such is the nature of metaphor, of the parables as metaphors, and of the underlying assumption in the Bible of how the divine and the human orders are related. But the particular *way* that the parable works the relation between the two dimensions is the crucial question, and it is on this that we must now focus. A parable, an extended metaphor, works the relation between the ordinary and the extraordinary in the same way as a metaphor. An allegory is translucent to its reality – it is a form of direct communication which assumes that the reader or listener already knows about the reality being symbolized. Metaphor, on the contrary, is indirect, attempting to bring about new insight by fram-ing the ordinary in an extraordinary context. That is to say, 'the certain shock to the imagination' is *seeing the familiar in a new way*; the stress in a parable is not seeing something completely unfamiliar, or something 'religious.' One does not see 'the divine' directly in a parable at all.

Thus in the parable of the Wedding Feast we are at no point 'taken out' of the story into a 'religious' world; the shock or new insight of the parable is in being brought to see that everyday situation – the wedding feast and its guest list – in a new way: invitation not by merit but by a gracious lack of concern about merit. The invitation by grace is brought to light, glimpsed, pointed to by means of cracks in the realism of the story – exaggeration, hyperbole, dislocations (the refusal of all the worthy guests to come, the shameful treatment and unmerited murder of the servants, the closing invitation to the people of the streets to come to the feast). The whole movement of the story not only is kept within its own confines at every point but returns the reader who would participate fully in it and be illuminated by it again and again to the story itself.

This is to say that as an indirect mode, metaphor does not, like discursive language, direct attention to 'the thing' but directs it elsewhere in such a way that 'the thing' is glimpsed. If this is the case, only fuller attention to the 'elsewhere' will provide further illumination of 'the thing.' Christianity is necessarily and always wedded to indirection. It is also a way of knowing which delimits spectator knowledge, primarily because what is being offered is not information one can store but an experience. It is a truism to say that art is not kinetic; it does not force anyone to make a decision, to *do* anything. Kierkegaard was right when he insisted on the hiatus between the aesthetic and the ethical, a hiatus that can be bridged only by an agent. But it is also true that those who have followed the movement of the two 'logics' of the parable of the Wedding Feast find themselves provoked, stimulated, edged into a decision about which 'logic' will be their own. In a sense, the parable has trapped them; it starts off on ordinary ground and catches them off balance as it switches 'logics' mid-way. The parable does not teach a spectator a lesson; rather it invites and surprises a participant into an experience. This is its power, its power then and now to be revelatory, not once upon a time, but every time a person becomes caught up in it and by it.

A parable of Jesus is not only an interesting story; it is a call to decision issued from one who in some way or other is himself a parable, or, as Christians believe, *the* parable of God. It is, then, not just another work of art; we have stressed the aesthetic nature of the parable not merely because parables have been debased into allegories and homilies but because of the religious significance of the aesthetic quality of parables. The crucial point is that a parable is metaphorical at every level and in every way – in language, in belief, in life. To say that it is metaphorical in language is obvious – the multitude of familiar images employed by the New Testament to evoke that great unfamiliar, the kingdom of God, needs little elaboration. The kingdom is never defined; it is spoken of in metaphorical language. But there is a deeper sense in which parables are metaphoric. A parable is an *extended* metaphor – the metaphor is not in discrete images which allow for a flash of insight (a purely aesthetic or intellectual 'Aha!'), but it is a way of believing and living that initially seems ordinary, yet is so dislocated and rent from its usual context that, if the parable 'works,' the spectators become participants, not because they want to necessarily or simply have 'gotten the point' but because they have, for the moment, 'lost control' or as the new hermeneuts say, 'been interpreted.' The secure, familiar everydayness of the story of their own lives has been torn apart; they have seen another story – the story of a mundane life like their own moving by a different 'logic,' and they begin to understand (not just with their heads) that another way of believing and living – another context or frame for their lives – might be a possibility *for them*.

The impact of the parables is directly tied to their qualities as aesthetic objects, their insistence that insight be embodied, incarnated; but the uncanny and unnerving aspect of the New Testament parables is that the peculiar insight they are concerned with, believing in a loving God who upsets the logic of the familiar, must be embodied, incarnated in human *lives*, not in the head alone but in and through the full scope and breadth of a human life. If this is the parabolic way it is necessarily metaphoric, necessarily indirect, because it is concerned not with what we believe, know, or are, but what we are in the process of believing, knowing, and becoming *in our lives*. Parables are not, then, riddles which give privileged knowledge to those who solve them. They are not *primarily* concerned with knowing but with doing (understood as deciding on a way of life based on new insight). Thus, to emphasize the parable as aesthetic object does not mean resting in whatever insight it may give us, but rather, while recognizing that its *power* to bring to decision derives from its aesthetic qualities, we must not forget that the goal of a parable is finally in the realm of willing, not of knowing.* In a parable we are, as Perrin says, confronted by Jesus' vision of reality and challenged to decide what we will do about it.

To read a parable of Jesus is ultimately to be confronted by Jesus' vision of reality. As an aid to this, we can and we should consider the nature and function of metaphor and of metaphorical language, we can and we should consider such literary aspects as the movement of the plot, the function of disclosure scenes, the Unjust Steward as a picaresque rogue, and so on. But ultimately what matters is the vision of reality of the author and the challenge of that vision of reality to ourselves.[15]

Parable and Theology

Throughout this discussion of parable as metaphor there has been the assumption that the parabolic form is not simply one of many literary forms used in the New Testament but a central one, if not *the* central one. We have rejected views of the parables as teaching devices, as moral illustrations, as allegories, and have stressed both the necessity of the parable as metaphor to Christianity, given the incarnation (however interpreted), and the outstanding trait of metaphor – its indirection, its curious wedding of realism and strangeness.

But more lies here than has been so far apparent. For what is implied in these comments is the uncovering of an ancient and authentic genre of theological reflection, a genre which suggests a significantly different mode of theological reflection than is evident in the dominant tradition of Western Christianity. Let me approach this very prickly question by repeating a tentative but highly provocative suggestion that Robert Funk has made by means of the following contrast:

---

* 'The analogies developed in parables are not just any analogies. They are those which help us to develop our policies for living and decide on their adoption. The central analogies are ones which suggest roles and rules in life, such as the role of sonship and the rule of neighbourly love. They are rarely analogies to impersonal features of the universe, designed to aid in speculating about anything as abstruse as "being as such"' (Peter Slater, 'Parables, Analogues and Symbols,' *Religious Studies*, 4 [1968], 27).

... the *Gattung* [genre] gospel tends to make *explicit* what is only *implicit* in the parable; and thus violates the intention of what may be the dominant mode of discourse in which Jesus taught. One could put it more incisively: the mystery of the kingdom held in solution in the parables precisely as mystery, tends to be profaned, made public, by the *Gattung* gospel. If we permit the 'gospel' to be defined by Jesus' parables, the question then arises: has the *Gattung* known as 'gospel' not already transgressed the intention of the 'gospel' defined as parable?[16]

If the parables are taken as the way to the 'gospel,' then Mark's messianic secret and John's figures and metaphors may be, in their own fashion, attempts to make their forms conform to the parable; concomitantly, the explicit tradition, the tradition that focuses on *kerygma*, on *didache*, deviates from such conformation.* Funk quotes the remark by Ebeling – 'the parable is the form of the language of Jesus which corresponds to the incarnation' – and then continues:

> We have come around . . . to the root theological problem: Does the *kerygma*, or the *kerygma* plus *didache*, faithfully mirror the 'gospel' as Jesus and his word, where Jesus and his word are taken to be embodied in pure form, in the parable? (Ebeling).[17]

Paul Ricoeur, following the lead of Amos Wilder, insists also that there is no way to the content of the Bible apart from its literary forms.

> The 'confession of faith' which is expressed in the biblical documents is inseparable from the *forms* of discourse. . . .the finished

---

* Helmut Koester and James M. Robinson (*Trajectories through Early Christianity* [Philadelphia: Fortress Press, 1971]), make the point that the *Gattung* gospel in the early church provided the necessary context for the interpretation of the parables, guarding against Gnostic misinterpretation of the parables as allegorical revelation by setting the parables within the context of an earthly human story. This is an important point for it suggests by implication that theology dependent on parable – what I am calling intermediary theology – and theology dependent on the gospel or kerygma, *both* have a crucial place in Christian reflection. It suggests that a metaphorical theology alone, apart from the more direct tradition of systematic theology, is liable to aberrations or obscurity. It is still my contention that the theological temper of our time is such that the form which holds the mystery in solution is more needed than the one that confronts it directly; but neither tradition can do without the other.

work which we call the Bible is a limited space for interpretation in which the theological significations are correlatives of forms of disclosure. It is no longer possible to interpret the significations without making the long detour through a structural explication of the forms.[18]

If the interdependence of form and content suggested by Funk, Ricoeur, and Wilder is taken with utmost seriousness, as I think it must be, then theological discourse, which has for the most part been discursive and conceptual, may well be in need of radical correction. If the parable (and its close cousins, story and confession) are seen as primary forms for theology, then the content of theology might well be different than it has been in the past.

We can approach this matter in a more concrete way. The key suggestion that Funk is making in the passages quoted above is that Jesus not only taught in parables but was himself the parable of God.* Leander Keck fleshes out Funk's point.

Just as the parable does not illustrate ideas better stated nonpara bolically, and so become dispensable, so Jesus is not merely an illustration for the kingdom which can be more adequately grasped apart from him – say in mystic encounters or in abstract formulations. His task was not to impart correct concepts about the kingdom but to make it possible for men to respond to it. . . .He not only tells shocking stories but leads a shocking life toward a shocking end. Just as the parables have familiar elements in unfamiliar plots, so Jesus' life has familiar features of Palestinian life in startling juxtapostion. . . .[19]

There are two central points in this statement: Jesus, as the parable of God, did not tell people about the kingdom but he *was* the kingdom; and the way his whole life brought people to the kingdom was through a juxtaposition of the ordinary within a startling new context. If theology is to be parabolic, it must attend very

___

* Or, as Leander Keck puts it, 'Jesus preferred parables not merely because there is an inner connection between the parabolic mode of speech and the mode and motive of his work. Jesus concentrated on parabolic speech because he himself was a parabolic event of the kingdom of God' (*A Future for the Historical Jesus: The Place of Jesus in Preaching and Theology* [Nashville: Abingdon Press, 1971], p. 244).

closely to these features; that is, it must not be concerned *primarily* with explaining and systematizing concepts about the kingdom but must look carefully at the way parables function, both the ones in the New Testament and Jesus as a parable. For, as Keck says, the goal of a parable is not 'to impart concepts about the kingdom but to make it possible for men to respond to it.' This, the possibility of response, is what we have called the task of theology – it is what contemporary theology calls 'hermeneutic.' It is the hearing of the word of God which results in acceptance, in faith, and the way this takes place, on the model of the parables and Jesus as the parable, is through imaginative participation.* It is a coming to a moment of insight when one's ordinary situation is seen in a new setting, a startling setting (called 'the coming of the kingdom' in the New Testament). This moment of insight is not a discrete mystical moment, but, again, if we take our clues from the parables, one that emerges from one's story and has implications for all of one's life.

It also has serious implications, as we have said, for theology. Intermediary or parabolic theology would attempt to unite form and content, to be in genre what it claims to be about. The suggestion may sound risky (which it is), but it is not novel, for it is the theological way of reflection not only of the first Christian theologian, Paul of Tarsus, but of a whole company of theologians up to and including some on the contemporary scene. We might include, to name a few, the Augustine of the *Confessions*, John Woolman, Luther, Schleiermacher, Jonathan Edwards, Kierkegaard, Teilhard de Chardin, and Bonhoeffer. These theologians share several characteristics, though not of course all to the same degree or with the same emphasis.

First, they use highly metaphorical *language*, aware that such

---

* '. . . it is clear that the failure of encounter with the New Testament is to be seen as much in the failure of imaginative participation as it is in the failure of loyalty. Those who are most consciously loyal to the faith expressed in the New Testament often fail to understand what the faith is. One reason for this failure arises from a situation which the New Testament shares with all other creative literature, namely, that its original impact was made by a "deformation" of language, a stretching of language to a new metaphorical meaning which shocked the hearer . . . into a new insight. With the course of time such "deformations" lose their newness, and often even their original metaphorical character, and become flat, commonplace words' (William A. Beardslee, *Literary Criticism of the New Testament* [Philadelphia: Fortress Press, 1970], pp. 10–11).

language is the way to bring their readers to insight, to confrontation with the word of God. Their vocabulary and style tends to be neither literalistically biblical nor highly abstract; much as poets utilize the common language to evoke the uncommon, these theologians use the metaphors and images of their particular culture, whether these be the Neoplatonic metaphors of light and dark or the evolutionary metaphors of groping and process. They do not abstract from these metaphors, attempting to explain or interpret them, but for the most part let them stay in solution. If they do systematic work it arises from and remains organically dependent on the metaphorical base.*

Secondly, they are concerned with the process of coming to *belief*. These metaphorical theologians are aware that what is at stake in Christianity is not belief in doctrines correctly stated, but 'believing,' a process which is more like a story than it is like a doctrine. As Richard R. Niebuhr says, 'Believing belongs to experience. . . .It arises in the times of testing in which human faithfulness takes shape and becomes tangible as an affection.'[20] Metaphor as the way human beings get from here to there, from, in this instance, unbelief to believing, is what theological reflection is about; it is not primarily about formulations and systems. Believing has a narrative quality, for it is a process, usually a slow process, which moves from the unsurprising to the surprising with the complexity and ambiguity, the stops and starts, the insights and the setbacks of a story.† The novel is a prime example of metaphor as method, of the gradual development and shaping of fully concrete beings toward believing perspectives of many varieties. The intermediary theologians take

* The fatherhood of God, for instance, is both a major metaphor and a major model in Western Christian thought. The development of a metaphor into a model is a movement from revelatory insight to the possibility of conceptual and systematic elaboration. Ian Barbour speaks of the distinction between metaphor and model in the following way: 'Metaphors are employed only momentarily . . . but models are more fully elaborated and serve as wider interpretive schemes in many contexts . . . models offer ways of ordering experience and of interpreting the world. . . .They lead to conceptually formulated, systematic, coherent religious beliefs which can be criticized, analyzed and evaluated' (*Myths, Models and Paradigms*, pp. 16, 27). An interesting and important exercise would be the analysis of major theological positions in terms of the dominant models they employ, for the difficult question of the way in which theology moves from primary religious images to systematic thought would be illuminated, I believe, by attention to such central models.

† For a superb discussion of this, see Stephen Crites, 'The Narrative Quality of Experience,' *Journal of the American Academy of Religion*, 39 (September 1971), 291–311.

with utmost seriousness the story quality of believing, and for this reason they focus on what carries the movement toward belief, the growing feeling or sense of confidence in the goodness of the power that rules the universe. It is at the level of what used to be called 'the affections,' the loves and fears and hopes that *move* one, that one's story takes place. It is here that Paul focuses in his hymn to love in I Cor. 13, Augustine in his concern with the two loves, Schleiermacher and Edwards with their concentration on human feeling, Teilhard de Chardin in his awareness of the active and passive phases of human life. Believing comes out of experience, out of one's story; Christian believing sees in the story of Jesus the metaphor of all believing, a life developing toward its consummation in death still believing that the ultimate power is worthy of trust.

Finally, then, such intermediary theologies, metaphorical in language and in belief, are also metaphorical in *life*. That is, in some fashion or other the life of the theologian is itself seen as a metaphor, a quite ordinary base for the operation of the extraordinary. Neither language nor belief can subsist except in a particular life, and our theologians are unabashedly autobiographical, not because they would boast of where they are in the pilgrimage toward believing but because they know that there is no such thing as disembodied, abstract theology. Paul, Augustine, Woolman, Luther, Kierkegaard, Bonhoeffer must, somehow or other, themselves *be* the 'human metaphor,' one partner in the association of the human with the transcendent. 'Confessional literature' has been a minor genre in Christian letters, but it ought to be a primary one if the metaphorical method is taken seriously, for where does one *start* to theologize if not with oneself?

The pain of this starting point is evident in Paul and Augustine and Woolman, for it involves looking at the deception and the inadequacies of one's own story of the attempt to be believing – to be believing not with one's head but in one's total life-style. Kierkegaard's sensitivity to the agony of becoming a Christian, Bonhoeffer's intuition of his own religionless Christianity, Teilhard's struggle to be an instrument in God's cosmic plan even in diminishment and death, are all intimations of what is at stake when the theologian's *own self* is taken as the human metaphor, the reflection of the inexpressible unfamiliar, the power and love of God. It is a daring and risky venture, open to misunderstanding and misuse, but if thought and life, knowing and being are to be one, if one dare not say with one's mouth what one does not attempt to embody in one's life, there is no other way.

What is coming into focus from our study of parables and of Jesus as the parable of God is a model for theological reflection that insists on the metaphoric quality of language, belief, and life. As I said in the Introduction, we discover the necessarily parabolic or metaphoric character of our confession, for Christian language must always be ordinary, contemporary, and imagistic (as it is in the parables); Christian belief must always be a process of coming to belief – like a story – through the ordinary details of historical life (as it is in the parables, though in a highly compressed way); Christian life must always be the bold attempt to put the words and belief into practice (as one is called to do in the parables). But what are the resources of parabolic theology? Are they only the parables and life of Jesus?

Our models are certainly in these sources, but there are others as well, both within Christian letters and outside of them, which are on a continuum with the parables and the life of Jesus as a parable. Intermediary or parabolic theology has never existed in a cultural vacuum. It has always been surrounded by and learned from those sources in Western letters most intimately involved in metaphor – poetry, the narrative tradition, and autobiography. The relations between Christianity and poetry, the novel, and autobiography are complex and symbiotic; they arose together and influenced each other so deeply that it is difficult if not impossible to separate them. Poets have found the primal metaphors and symbols of the Christian tradition to be a major source for the expression of their own meanings; novelists, as Erich Auerbach and others have pointed out, have relied heavily on Christianity's insistence on the importance of human growth for the pattern of character development; Augustine is universally acclaimed as the first great autobiographer, and in significant ways all great autobiographies have followed his lead. Likewise, intermediary theologians have often looked to poets both to renew Christian symbols and to understand better how insight occurs through language, to novelists for deeper perception into the narrative character of the movement toward believing, to the autobiographical form for a way of grasping the interpenetration of life and thought. In poetry they have found metaphoric transformation of ordinary and contemporary language; in novels, metaphors of coming to belief; and in autobiographies, lives lived as metaphors – all on a continuum with the parables. In each case the ordinary is seen in a new context which transforms it. In such forms we are not 'told about' Christian language, belief, and life (as we are not in the parables or the story of Jesus), but we are invited to participate imaginatively in a new way of speaking, believing, and living, invited to contemplate some metaphors.

One of the major tasks, I believe, of contemporary theology is to struggle with metaphorical precision, and it is a difficult one. One does not move easily from poetic forms to discursive discourse, for metaphor is not finally translatable or paraphrasable. No literary critic would attempt to translate or paraphrase the 'content' of a Shakespearean sonnet: it could not be done and it would be a travesty if attempted. The critic who does not attempt to keep his or her method and language close to the sonnet, who does not attempt to bring others to the experience of the poem, may write an interesting book or article, but it will not have much to do with the sonnet. He or she may turn out to be an aesthetician or a philosopher, but this is to move into another mode entirely – that of discursive language.

And this brings us to an interesting point. Is the theologian more like the aesthetician and philosopher or more like the literary critic?* Is it his or her job to create a system which explains, interprets, and organizes the primary data or is it to help the preacher, to help people to hear the word of God today? I think it is the latter, though I am not denying the necessity of the former task as well. But its predominance in the last few centuries has eclipsed what is to my

* On this point H. Richard Niebuhr makes the following comment: '. . . theology is related to faith somewhat as literary criticism is related to poetic action and expression. Here again participation is indispensable. The literary critic must know by direct participation what the aesthetic experience is, what the poetic creation requires in the way of both inspiration and labor, and what sort of movement takes place in the poet's mind between sensuous symbol and meaning. . . .The theological critic is in a similar situation. Without participation in the life of faith he cannot distinguish between its high and low, genuine and spurious experiences and expressions, between symbol and meaning. But as the work of literary critics presupposes and is ancillary to the work of poets, so the activity of theologians is secondary to that of believers' (*Radical Monotheism and Western Culture* [New York: Harper and Brothers, 1960], p. 15).

mind the primary task of the theologian – reflecting theologically in ways that keep Christian language, believing, and life close to its primary model, the parable, so that, like the parable, it helps people to be encountered by the word of God.

Part II

5

The Poem:
Language of Insight

If theology were to be truly parabolic in language, belief, and life, what would it be like? Would it be itself a parable? Perhaps. But I suspect that theological attempts to be faithful to the parabolic model will be necessarily more partial and diffuse. A parabolic theology locates its sources not in doctrines and systems but in what lies behind doctrine and systems — in language, belief, and life-styles that have attempted to be metaphors of Christian faith. We are concerned here with the *resources* of intermediary theology, with what theologians might attend to were they concerned, not to be poets, on the one hand, or systematic theologians, on the other. We are concerned with their effort to be metaphoric in their reflection, staying close to the parabolic form with its insistence on using common language in novel ways to evoke insight, with its emphasis on the narrative quality of believing, its foundation in experience, and with both language and belief rooted in a total life-style. The kind of theologies that might emerge from attention to such sources will not be poems, novels, or autobiographies, but they will be significantly formed by these sources.*

---

* A brief illustration of how the parabolic mode would deal with one question – the person and work of Jesus Christ – might be illuminating. As all know, the Council of Nicaea and the long theological debate that ensued, which dealt with the internal relations of the Trinity, preceded the Councils of Ephesus and Chalcedon, which dealt with the person and work of Jesus Christ. Having already determined precisely and conceptually the substantiality of the Logos, or second person of the Trinity, the Fathers apparently believed they had little choice when they got around to dealing with Jesus but to equate his 'person' with the hypostasis of the Logos, and we have never since been able in good conscience to affirm his full humanity with all that it implies. The agency, the person, what have you, is *really* the Logos; and Barth in the twentieth century, in spite of his nods to the historical story of Jesus, ends up with Ephesus and Chalcedon. What might have been the case, however, if the

The parabolic way of doing theology means being open to sources of funding that the Church has not always taken very seriously. When theologians speak of 'the tradition,' they usually mean the doctrinal tradition – the Councils of the Church and the great theologians. But if the parabolic way is taken seriously, its sources cannot possibly reside in doctrine, for doctrine is the sedimentation of metaphors, it is the agreed-upon understanding of the images, and as agreed upon such images are already dead or dying.

But more specifically, what does it mean to say that theology should find its sources in poetry, novels, and autobiographies? It means many things, as we shall see, but with regard to poetry, for instance, it means a deformation of traditional symbols of Christianity, a placing of the symbols in new contexts, so that they may again become metaphors, become revelatory. Christian poets throughout the ages have helped people to participate imaginatively in Christian language – in other words, have helped them to hear the word of God – by placing the imagistic language of the tradition in fresh contexts so that the dead metaphors may become alive once more. As Beardslee says, the original impact of the New Testament was made 'by a "deformation" of language, a stretching of language to a new metaphorical meaning which shocked the hearer into new insight. With the course of time such "deformations" lose their newness, and often even their original metaphorical character, and become flat, commonplace words.'[1] When this occurs, only metaphor can recreate the possibility for revelatory participation. This is not merely a question of translating old symbols into a modern idiom, but the more basic hermeneutical task of suggesting new contexts – strange and extraordinary ones – for language that has become ordinary and flat that it may live again. For the goal is not simply the 'renewal' of traditional symbols but, more radically, the creation of an encounter situation which will, as Wilder says, give 'that

---

parabolic way of understanding had been followed? If Chalcedon had preceded Nicaea, or if the Church Fathers had turned to the biblical story of Jesus instead of Nicaea and Ephesus for their moorings, they might have been faced with and had to deal with the mystery, ambiguity, indirection, in other words, the parabolic quality of an actual human life and its growth. The final doctrinal formulation of the person and work of Jesus Christ would have come out very differently. It would at least have been less metaphysical, more secular; less literal, more suggestive; less allegorical, more metaphorical.

certain shock to the imagination,' helping people to say 'Yes,' not simply with their heads, but with commitment to be lived out in their entire lives.

With regard to the novel, intermediary theology finds a source for the recreation of the Scriptural insistence on the narrative quality of coming to belief. The story of Jesus, Paul's confessions, and even the creeds are narratives, for Christian belief is a story of what God has done and how we respond to his action. It takes place in and through the stuff of ordinary life; belief is a temporal and historical process, suggesting that intermediary or parabolic theology should be written as a story, not as a treatise. Christian novels tell stories of coming to belief – they are metaphors creating new contexts, contemporary contexts, for that old possibility, and thus allowing us to participate imaginatively and immediately in that possibility. The parables are the primary models here, but there are novels which are parabolic in form, not talking about belief but showing people coming to belief.

In autobiographies, finally, intermediary theology has a source for understanding how language and belief move into a life, how a life can itself *be* a parable, a deformation of ordinary existence by its placement in an extraordinary context. The letters of Paul or the *Confessions* of Augustine recreate existentially and personally the heart of the parables and the story of Jesus – what it means to live an ordinary, historical life in the surprising context of God's grace. We are invited to participate imaginatively in the old story now told once again through the joints and ligaments of a particular human life story.

But is it only *Christian* poetry, novels, and autobiographies that are sources for intermediary theologians? We shall concentrate on these sources because form and content are so intricately linked that it is questionable if we can have one without the other. It is false, I believe, to separate form and content to such an extent that one calls whatever appears 'good' or 'religious' or concerned with the 'transcendent' in a poem, novel, or autobiography 'Christian.'* Yet, as we have indicated in the previous chapter, Christianity and the literary forms we are dealing with grew up together and mutually influenced each other. Thus there are poets, novelists, and autobiographers who, although not Christian, have been so deeply influenced by

* For a fuller treatment of this point see Ch. 1 of my book, *Literature and the Christian Life* (New Haven: Yale University Press, 1971).

the parabolic mode – the hidden way of locating the graciousness of the universe within the ordinary and the mundane – that their works are, indeed, sources for the intermediary theologian. While form cannot finally be separated from content, theologians can sometimes find within so-called 'secular' literature the parabolic *form*, and we shall look briefly at the work of a few of these artists. In the poetry of Denise Levertov or the novels of J. R. R. Tolkien, for instance, one does find the deformation of ordinary life through its placement in new and gracious contexts. In fact, one often learns the most from these 'anonymous Christians' (as Karl Rahner would call them), for if they are consummate artists as well as deeply parabolic they can show, in a way that a nominal Christian artist who is mediocre cannot, how hidden and yet how powerful the parabolic way is.

Christian Poetry

One distinctive note of Christian poetry is its personal focus. As Amos Wilder puts it:

> The Gospel's story-forms, however artistic, have a formidable personal focus which distinguish them. Its poem-forms, similarly, focus upon the heart and its ultimate response to God.[2]

The Davidic psalms, of course, manifest the same quality:

> O Lord my God, in thee do I take refuge;
> Save me from all my pursuers, and deliver me,
> Lest like a lion they rend me,
> Dragging me away, with none to rescue.
>
> (Psalm 7:1–2)

> The Lord is my shepherd, I shall not want. . . .
>
> (Psalm 23:1)

> Bless the Lord, O my soul;
> And all that is within me,
> Bless his holy name!
>
> (Psalm 103:1)

Likewise in Luke's Magnificat, the perspective is personal: 'My soul magnifies the Lord, / and my spirit rejoices in God my Savior.' There are, of course, some traditions where the epic is the outstanding poetic form – one thinks of Homer and of Virgil. There are also strong epic qualities in the Old Testament stories. But Christian poetry, by and large, when most successful, has been lyric. The *Divine Comedy* and *Paradise Lost* stand counter to this statement, but we must not forget that the epic episodes of the *Divine Comedy* are held together by the personal, existential focus of Dante as the chief character in the poem, or that literary opinion on *Paradise Lost* finds the greatest interest and literary success not in the epic heavenly warfare but in the personal tragedy of Satan.

The lyric form, then, seems to be a highly appropriate Christian form, and it is not very difficult, given what has already been said about the parable, to figure out why. A lyric poem is a highly personal metaphorical expression. It is a form of deep personal engagement, as is the parable, engagement to the point of creating a radically new context for traditional symbols. There are as many ways of going about this as there are Christian poets, for what a lyric poem offers is a *personal* focus, and what we get from various poems is what Philip Wheelwright calls 'perspectival individuality' on reality.[3] The 'reality' which is deformed, given a new context, through 'perspectival individuality' by Christian poets is, of course, the good news of the New Testament. Christianity is not just *anything* that is serious or 'ultimate'; it has a Gestalt which is carried poetically in images, symbols, and stories from the tradition. The Gestalt is recognizable even when the symbols are radically transformed through metaphorical power (as in G. M. Hopkins' metaphor of the death of a windhover to evoke Jesus' crucifixion). It is also recognizable when no such traditional clues are given, as in Eliot's 'Burnt Norton' where 'the moment in the rose-garden' is the vehicle of the incarnational thrust of the poem – 'Only through time time is conquered.'

The 'test' of a *Christian* poet is whether or not the reality with which he or she is dealing is the transformation or recontextualization of the ordinary by the graciousness of God. It is not impossible to separate the Christian poets who have been concerned with this process from those who merely use Christian symbols because they provide a rich tradition for their own perspective. Genuine Christian poets fall back on those untranslatable root metaphors – the images, symbols, and stories in Scripture. They are our signposts which help us to read our way and for which the poet must provide new contexts, create new metaphors, in order that they may be read at all. It is extraordinarily difficult to be a Christian poet, for it involves both motions simultaneously: reading the signs by transforming them. We will look at some examples of metaphoric recreation of traditional Christian themes and images; the examples are highly selective and are intended to be illustrations only. The main point is to show that 'perspectival individuality' can renovate, make new, create new contexts that dead metaphors and symbols may live again.

HOLY SONNET 5

I am a little world made cunningly
Of elements, and an angelic sprite;
But black sin hath betrayed to endless night
My world's both parts, and oh, both parts must die.
You which beyond that heaven which was most high
Have found new spheres, and of new lands can write,
Pour new seas in mine eyes, that so I might
Drown my world with my weeping earnestly,
Or wash it if it must be drowned no more.
But oh, it must be burnt? Alas, the fire
Of lust and envy have burnt it heretofore,
And made it fouler; let their flames retire
And burn me, O Lord, with a fiery zeal
Of Thee and Thy house, which doth in eating heal.[4]

John Donne's sonnet is a tightly woven fabric, highly economical and highly metaphoric. The octet sets the problem in narrative fashion: the speaker tells his story through the metaphor of worlds. *He* is a world, composed of matter and spirit, but a world in which it is always night because of his sin. 'Creation,' the world that he is, is not only in constant darkness, but must die. The individual perspective is dominant but it is carried entirely through the metaphor of 'world,' and harkens back to the goodness of creation ('cunningly,' 'angelic sprite'). The microcosm-macrocosm metaphor is continued in l.5 as attention shifts to the creator who knows of 'new spheres' and 'new lands' and from whom the speaker hopes for renewal – 'pour new seas in mine eyes.' The point of view in ll.7–8 is still self-pitying: the plea for 'new seas' is to destroy himself with weeping. In 1.9, the beginning of the sestet, a slight shift is evident at 'Or wash it,' recalling the possibilities of baptismal washing, and in l.10 the self-pity dramatically shifts to a decision for renewal through fire. The strong narrative quality in this sonnet is reminiscent of the dramatic reversals in Jesus' parables, in the Prodigal Son, for instance. The pace is fast in the last five lines as the contrasting metaphors of the fires of lust and envy and the purifying fires which 'in eating heal' tumble over one another. The extremity of the speaker's situation is clinched in these final three words which contrast sharply with the relaxed opening line of the sonnet and the earlier suggestion that weeping might take care of the situation.

This sonnet is deeply metaphorical: its meaning is carried by the subtle interplay of the metaphors of world and worlds (and the accompanying structural metaphors of matter and spirit, darkness and night, seas, drowning, new lands) and of water and fire (and the accompanying structural metaphors of washing, eating, and healing). It is an extremely complex meditation on death and renewal, a peculiarly pat one for cultural and scientific seventeenth-century England, but not unavailable to us. The meaning of the metaphors is ingredient, of course, to their interplay and movement within the poem, to the associations they suggest, to the participation of the reader which they invite. There is no way to get at the meaning of the poem in any other way, no way to reduce it to a set of assertions: the meaning is held 'in solution' and that solution is the poem itself. As metaphoric discourse, it invites contemplation, not extrapolation. It provides us with a set of familiar terms in which to glimpse the unfamiliar and in glimpsing it through worlds, water, and fire, we see it anew.

But it is in the same universe as the parables of Jesus; it is concerned with the same issues and is concerned with them in the same way – individually and parabolically. The ethos of the poem is Christian, not because 'religious' language is used but because two logics of understanding everyday personal reality are operative, the logic, in this instance, of self-pity, on the one hand, and the logic of acceptance of unmerited renewal, on the other. It is, I believe, a Christian poem.

THE FLOWER

How fresh, O Lord, how sweet and clean
Are Thy returns! Even as the flowers in spring,
    To which, besides their own demean,
The late-past frosts tributes of pleasure bring.
        Grief melts away
        Like snow in May,
As if there were no such cold thing.

Who would have thought my shriveled heart
Could have recovered greenness? It was gone
    Quite underground, as flowers depart
To see their mother-root, when they have blown;
        Where they together
        All the hard weather,
Dead to the world, keep house unknown.

These are Thy wonders, Lord of power,
Killing and quickening, bringing down to hell
    And up to heaven in an hour;
Making a chiming of a passing-bell.
        We say amiss
        This or that is;
Thy word is all, if we could spell.

O that I once past changing were,
Fast in Thy paradise, where no flower can wither!
    Many a spring I shoot up fair,
Offering at heaven, growing and groaning thither;
        Nor doth my flower
        Want a spring shower,
My sins and I joining together.

But while I grow in a straight line,
Still upwards bent, as if heaven were mine own,
    Thy anger comes, and I decline.
What frost to that? What pole is not the zone
        Where all things burn,
        When Thou dost turn,
And the least frown of Thine is shown?

And now in age I bud again;
After so many deaths I live and write;
  I once more smell the dew and rain,
And relish versing. O my only Light,
    It cannot be
    That I am he
On whom Thy tempests fell all night.

These are Thy wonders, Lord of love,
To make us see we are but flowers that glide;
  Which when we once can find and prove,
Thou hast a garden for us where to bide.
    Who would be more,
    Swelling through store,
Forfeit their paradise by their pride.[5]

George Herbert's poem 'The Flower' is, metaphorically, very different from Donne's sonnet. One metaphor predominates and many combinations are rung on it. The tone is more casual, more relaxed; it is seemingly effortless, but the movement of death and rebirth, despair and self-hope, confidence and humility are as ingredient in these metaphors as in Donne's. The dominant imagery of natural renewal in seasonal life is the vehicle which carries the meditative movement of the poem. The first verse sets the contrasts of 'sweet and clean' returns and the 'late-past frosts' which run throughout the poem. The wonder of natural renewal is mirrored in the speaker's personal experience of the second verse with the marvelous immediacy of the metaphor of the 'shriveled heart' recovering 'greenness.'

Every succeeding line in the poem modifies and enriches the central metaphor of renewal. The third stanza moves from the personal to a general reflection on the 'killing and quickening' power of the 'Lord of power,' who controls nature (stanza 1) and every individual (stanza 2). Stanzas 4 and 5 are autobiographical, the story of a proud man who wants to be past the constant fluctuations of temporal life, to make his offerings, to grow in a straight line – storming heaven with his healthy sins well-watered. But in stanza 5, ll.3–4, the frost metaphor is picked up again and the movement appears of stretching and declining, killing and quickening, growing heavenward and retreating underground which the speaker has been working throughout the poem. The resolution begins in stanza 6 and continues to the end in the same metaphors as used throughout the poem: bud, smell, dew, light, tempests, flowers. The acceptance of lowly status – 'but flowers that glide' – is possible because he can once more 'smell the dew and rain / And relish versing.' Not paradise, but the ability to do and love very human, sensuous, ordinary things (which for a poet includes writing poems!) is what his greenness and budding is all about.

The language of this poem may be 'religious' but the renewal he seeks and finds is not; in fact, he repudiates the attempt to 'fast in Thy paradise' as inappropriate. The metaphors in the poem keep the wonder of renewal firmly fixed on ordinary human experience: the new life has to do with dew and rain and versing. It is a highly sensuous poem and the new context for the language of pride and acceptance which it offers is in precisely those terms. The life cycle of a flower is the vehicle for the recreation of the Church's language of sin and grace: the familiar sensuous imagery lets us participate imaginatively in those realities. The extended metaphor of the flower does not *illustrate* sin and grace; rather, the complex meanings of the metaphor throughout the poem are what allows us to *see them at all*. Another way to say it is that without the flower metaphor we would have a few banal assertions about God's power to control us; the medium, in this instance the flower metaphor and its many interplays, is the meaning.

THE WINDHOVER:
To Christ our Lord

I caught this morning morning's minion, king-
　dom of daylight's dauphin, dapple-dawn-drawn Falcon, in his
　　riding
Of the rolling level underneath him steady air, and striding
High there, how he rung upon the rein of a wimpling wing
In his ecstasy! then off, off forth on swing,
　As a skate's heel sweeps smooth on a bow-bend: the hurl
　　and gliding
Rebuffed the big wind. My heart in hiding
Stirred for a bird, – the achieve of, the mastery of the thing!

Brute beauty and valour and act, oh, air, pride, plume here
   Buckle! AND the fire that breaks from thee then, a billion
Times told lovelier, more dangerous, O my chevalier!

   No wonder of it: sheer plod makes plough down sillion
Shine, and blue-bleak embers, ah my dear,
   Fall, gall themselves, and gash gold-vermilion.[6]

The only clue in G. M. Hopkins' poem that the windhover is a
metaphor of the crucifixion is in the subtitle, but the clue is not
necessary, even if one were to approach this poem cold and knew
nothing of the poet. For the poem 'works,' all by itself; it lets the
reader glimpse a pattern of majesty broken which is a parable, for
any Western consciousness, of the passion of Christ. There is, let
us note at the outset, no religious language in the poem: the images
are secular (horses, plume, rein, kingdom, dauphin, skate, plough)
and natural (daylight, air, wind, earth). This poem is, more than
the other two we have looked at, strictly parabolic, strictly indirect.
We are invited to experience the flight of a magnificent, powerful,
graceful bird who crumbles in flight (is he shot? blown against the
rocks? did the speaker kill him?) and whose death is more lovely and
more dangerous than his flight. The poem is an excellent example of
metaphorical precision, for the kind of precision achieved here is in
direct proportion to the complexity and richness of the imagery. By
piling complex image upon complex image, Hopkins drives toward
the 'inscape' or particularity of the bird's majestic flight and brilliant
death; that is, the most indirect path is the most direct, or to put
it differently, the only way to express radical particularity is through
a plethora of images juxtaposed to one another, sparking the imagination to move toward a synthesis which, while not logical, is, taken
as a whole, suggestive of a particularity.

What are some of the components of this particularity? The poem
is divided into three parts, which we might call the situation, the
crisis, and a reflection on both; these parts are indicated by the
paragraph breaks. The first part describes the incredibly free and
majestic flight of the bird in terms of an early morning vision: the
metaphors are drawn from three main sources – the light and wind
of early morning (daylight, dawn, air, wind), royalty (minion, falcon,
kingdom, dauphin), and horsemanship (riding, rein). The immediate

impression is one of power, nobility, speed, grace, beauty. This impression is fortified by the rhythm of the lines: 'Of the rolling level underneath him steady air' falls off the tongue with a smooth glide that exactly mirrors what the words are saying. In fact, this poem is so magnificently made that the *pattern* of majestic freedom and violent death can be sensed simply from the rhythm of the words apart from their meaning.

The spiraling, gliding bird suddenly buckles; we are not told why, but the opening 'I caught' suggests that the speaker's actions are involved. *What* buckles is complex: 'brute beauty,' 'plume,' and 'air' but also 'valour,' 'act,' and 'pride,' both the natural and human are involved; in fact, it takes on cosmic proportions. The surprising twist here, of course, is that the death of the bird is more magnificent than its flight.

The final reflection is a parable within the parable: even as the earth shines more richly when plowed and embers from a fire turn gold and red when they fall; so – the death of the bird is more brilliant, more lovely, and more dangerous than its life. Something shining, something beautiful comes out of the death of natural things.

No more is said and no more is necessary. The poem is a *parable* of the crucifixion, not an illustration of it, and as a parable it must be held in solution. It is in the tradition of Mark's messianic secret and John's 'signs,' not in the tradition of the gospel genre, the direct, discursive kerygma. What one learns from this poem about the crucifixion is the sort of learning which it is impossible to state discursively, but it is not esoteric. Just the opposite: it is available to anyone who spends time engaged with the poem (and a good dictionary) and it is immediate, participatory learning that allows one to enter imaginatively into the crucifixion, in almost unlimited ways. There is no way of exhausting the significance of the poem's possibility of helping us to encounter the crucifixion, just as there is no way of exhausting the understanding ingredient in all primal language, for the associations of metaphorical language are infinite.

The kind of recreation of Christian language which is emerging from our study of Christian poetry goes something like this: poetry does not illustrate meaning, it creates it, and Christian poetry creates meanings clustered around that complex we call the gospel. There is an infinite number of ways of approaching that complex indirectly, and probably no way of approaching it directly this side of heaven; the New

Testament images and stories serve as a rough guide to keep us from calling everything that is merely hopeful or positive 'Christian,' and to make it clear that such phenomena as racism and Manichaeism are definitely out. But the problems of discriminating between what is and is not Christian are less acute than the problem of the dessicated imagination, the problem of the abyss between the word of God and our imaginative appropriation of it. It is to this problem that poetic metaphor speaks, for the poetic imagination makes connections undreamt of by our impoverished imaginations. T. S. Eliot puts it this way:

> When a poet's mind is perfectly equipped for his work, it is consistently amalgamating disparate experiences; the ordinary man's experience is chaotic, irregular, fragmentary. The latter falls in love, or reads Spinoza, and these two experiences have nothing to do with each other, or with the noise of the typewriter or the smell of cooking; in the mind of the poet, these experiences are already forming new wholes.[7]

The ability to connect this with that, to make the jumps, to see the part as a whole, to *associate*, is the clue, I believe, that poetic metaphor suggests. Theologians, trained to see philosophical statement as the model for theology, often manifest mindsets that are univocal and literalistic. If we take the lessons of poetic metaphor seriously, theological training ought to include as a major component the development of the imagination. This does not mean, of course, that theologians need be poets. But those who work to help others to hear the word of God need to be radically open to associations with that word, which of course means assuming the risk of being wrong. To suggest associations which will help people encounter the word of God in contemporary images is a precarious undertaking and a highly uncomfortable one, but the alternative is a dead language and a ghettoized Christianity. It also means being aware of imaginative associations wherever they occur, and often this will involve cultural discomfort for the theologian, for the center of metaphorical renewal of Christian language in our time is often not among Christian poets but in popular culture and in 'secular' artists.

The three examples of metaphoric recreation in popular culture we shall look at briefly – folk hymns, the rock opera *Jesus Christ Superstar*, and Corita Kent's 'play-prayers' – have at least two qualities in common. They are all mixed genres, McLuhanesque in their impact, which suggests, I believe, an appreciation for the sensuous and the celebrative which has often been lacking, particularly in Protestant circles. They are liturgical forms, demanding a strong degree of audience participation and manifesting a lack of concern for purity of form. They have the vigor of popular culture as well as its transiency, and both qualities are to be applauded rather than deplored, for they express the vitality of the form. The introduction to a collection of folk hymns says of them:

> All speak of today, for today, to today. That's what's important. That's why they are here. They're for now. Which means they are to be used. Which means learn them. Hum them. Sing them. Whistle them. Strum them. Put them in the pew racks in church. Pile them in your guitar case. Toss them into the car. Throw them away when they wear out. Because by then there will be new ones.[8]

The casual, mixed confusion of popular Christian lyrical expression is a phenomenon which is indirect evidence that the great Christian symbols and stories are capable of metaphoric recreation and this alone, apart from their aesthetic and theological significance is noteworthy.

The second characteristic which these three mixed genres share is a similarity in the kind of metaphor they use. Philip Wheelwright makes a very useful distinction between two kinds of metaphor – metaphor of association or transference (epiphor) and metaphor of juxtaposition (diaphor).[9] The former is the classical type: the transference of a word from what it usually means to some other object, as in 'the milk of human kindness,' or 'God the Father.' The ability to employ this sort of metaphor, however, seems to rest on a confidence that things really *are* associated, that the center holds, that the web is not broken – that, in other words, the universe is in some sense sacramental, that God is somehow the true and original father, that all things are connected among themselves because they are connected in God. It depends, as C. Day-Lewis says, on believing that the human mind can claim 'kinship with everything that lives or has lived,'[10] or, as Paul Ricoeur puts it, 'it is an index of the situation of man at the heart of the being in which he moves, exists, and wills, that the symbol speaks to us.'[11] In significant ways, this sense of the unity of the human with all that is, is still part of our culture, and heightened ecological and mystical awareness has increased it for many. But it is not, I believe, the dominant sensibility in Christian circles, at least among those attempting to create new contexts for Christian symbols and stories. That is to say, the Christian symbolic universe does *not* hold together for most of us; the transference of the traditional Christian imagery to our situation today is not easy or natural; it is not an integral transference. We do not, like Bunyan's Pilgrim, see ourselves as reflecting, imitating, taking upon ourselves the biblical or other traditional symbols and stories and making them our own through transference.

The other kind of metaphor, juxtaposition, is particularly pertinent to the modern consciousness, for, alienated and disbelieving as we are, we respond to the ambiguity, irony, and covert cynicism of metaphorical juxtaposition. Wheelwright quotes the following extreme examples of new meaning by juxtaposition.

> My country 'tis of thee
> Sweet land of liberty
> > Higgledy-piggledy my black hen.

> The apparition of these faces in the crowd;
> Petals on a wet, black bough.[12]

The connections are not spelled out; two images are simply juxtaposed and the reader is left to make his or her own connections, though the choice of images juxtaposed of course delimits meaning in a certain direction. The contrasts are admittedly disjunctive, but they are endemic to the nature of metaphor, which Coleridge defined as the 'reconciliation of discordant or opposite qualities.' The 'reconciliation' aspect is more prevalent in metaphor of association, the 'discordant or opposite qualities' more evident in metaphor of juxtaposition, but both are crucial. In fact, most successful metaphors, such as these two by Shakespeare, are an indissoluble blend of both.

> > > my salad days,
> > When I was green in judgment.

> A bracelet of bright hair about the bone.

It is not possible to separate the two kinds of metaphor in any clear or absolute way, but it seems to me that contemporary Christian attempts rely heavily on metaphor by juxtaposition. Such reliance could be explained entirely by our alienation and disbelief, and I think that is part of it; lacking a sense of the unity of the Christian universe of symbols and stories, and of how such a universe might be ingredient in our universe, juxtaposition is the only alternative. Thus in *Jesus Christ Superstar* Herod says to Jesus: 'Prove to me that you're no fool / Walk across my swimming pool.'

But I think there is a more important, and a basically right-minded attitude manifest in the use of juxtaposition by Christians. The parables are by and large juxtapositions; when Jesus replied to a question by telling a parable, he did not make the connections. He simply juxtaposed a question with a story, and often a story with its own internal paradoxes. No attempt is made to systematize, to make connections between two 'universes' (a religious and a secular one), to take the hearer out of his or her world. Just the opposite: the effect of the juxtaposition is to focus on the significance of the hearer's world, to break intellectual or systematic connections in order to press toward personal, historic decisions. There is a sense in which the mystical, sacramental tradition enables the connections to be made too easily, too intellectually, too 'religiously.' The kind of new meaning that the form of the parables suggests militates against merely mental connections, insisting that the 'meaning' is not new unless it is existential meaning, meaning for actual individuals in their concrete historical and social circumstances. Such meaning will necessarily be somewhat hidden and ambiguous, for human meaning, unlike systematic meaning, is dense with mystery.

One must be careful here and not say too much. I am not suggesting that the tendency toward juxtaposed metaphor on the contemporary scene is conscious or entire, or that the associative metaphor we saw in Donne, Herbert, and Hopkins is false or passé.* But a more integrative Christian sensibility did exist for

---

* Most of the metaphors we shall look at function by association as well as by juxtaposition; in fact, pure juxtaposition verges on nonsense (the 'My country 'tis of thee' example). As one critic has said of the reliance of Wheelwright's diaphor on epiphor: 'The net effect of diaphor is to increase the possibility of pluri-signification by forcing the reader to create a relationship or a number of relationships, more or less cognitive, without finally insisting on a particular version' (David M. Miller,

Donne, Herbert, and Hopkins, and their achievement was magnificent: the union of the two kinds of metaphor is perfectly displayed in Hopkins' 'Windhover' and one marvels at such a poem. Such a sensibility does not exist widely now and it would be false to press for it. But what does exist now, the ability to juxtapose this with that, bread and wine with Wonder Bread ('helps build strong bodies 12 ways'),[13] is, I believe, genuinely biblical not only in form but also in content, for it opposes mystical and religious tendencies that thrive at the expense of social and secular ones.

Folk hymns are not great poetry and they are not intended as such by their authors. They are meant to be used and thrown away. Some are merely pious, as Christian hymnody is always prone to be, and some merely mimic traditional symbols, offering little metaphoric transformation. Some are message-oriented ('Jesus gave a new command / That we love our fellow man / Till we reach the promised land, / Where we'll live forever'). Many, it seems to me, rely too heavily on strong association where it no longer exists: there is a disappointing use of unmodified traditional Christian language ('God said he would send his Son, Allelu, Allelu! / And salvation would be won, Alleluia!'). The music is often first-rate – catchy, rhythmic, and exuberant – and I suspect it is this which carries the often mediocre lyrics. But some are genuinely metaphoric, and the most effective ones depend in part on metaphor of juxtaposition.

> They hung him in Jerusalem,
> And in Hiroshima,
> In Dallas and in Selma too,
> And in South Africa.[14]

> We hear you, O Man, in agony cry,
> For freedom you march, in riots you die.
> Your face in the papers we read and we see,
> The tree must be planted by human decree.[15]

The metaphoric impact is not overwhelming in these examples, but by a combination of association and juxtaposition of the agonizing

---

The Net of Hephaestus: A Study of Modern Criticism and Metaphysical Metaphor [The Hague: Mouton and Co., 1971], p. 113).

events of our time with symbols pointing to Jesus, imaginative encounter with his story becomes possible. What is important in the movement of folk hymnody is probably less the individual classics that may emerge (there will probably be few) than the impact upon our sensibility from the sheer quantity of songs which make a multitude of connections, often only fleeting and disjointed, between our times and the story of Jesus. Every time a person can see, even if only ironically and ambiguously, the events of his or her social and personal life illuminated by some aspect of the life and death of Jesus, then parabolic understanding is taking place, the ordinary is seen in a new context.

The metaphoric potential of the rock opera *Jesus Christ Superstar* is far greater.[16] It is a complex piece, and so dependent on its musical setting, which is eclectically rich, that a treatment of the libretto alone is something of a travesty. Nevertheless the libretto is extremely interesting in itself from a metaphorical perspective, for there are at least three sorts of material in the opera that use juxtaposition. One constellation of material is the person of Jesus – 'Jesus Christ Superstar – tell us that you're who they say you are.' The Jesus mania of the crowd is juxtaposed with the very human, even pathetic self-understanding of Jesus: 'There is not a man among you who knows or cares if I come or go,' and the poignant rephrasing of the words of institution, 'For all you care this wine could be my blood; / For all you care this bread could be my body.' The sentimental 'Touch me touch me Jesus / Jesus I am on your side' of the crowd and the inflated 'Hey JC, JC won't you smile at me? / Sanna Ho Sanna Hey Superstar' is juxtaposed with Jesus screaming at the moneylenders in the temple and the irresolute agony of the Gethsemane scene ('Show me there's a reason for your wanting me to die / You're far too keen on where and how and not so hot on why'). The juxtapositions are at times irreverently funny, and for these very reasons are highly effective indirect means of manifesting what has seldom been accomplished in literary renditions of the passion story – the humanity of Jesus. Jesus in Kazantzakis' *The Greek Passion* and in Faulkner's *A Fable* is a stick figure, marred only physically in the first (by a leprous rash on his face), distant and ethereal in the second. By the juxtaposition of the 'high Christology' represented by the crowd with the fighting, loving, distraught, irresolute Jesus of the narrative, new significance is generated. The 'symbol' Jesus Christ takes on flesh and blood, which only twice in the libretto is conceptualized: Mary Magdelene and Judas alone realize 'He's a man, he's just a man,' though there is something about him, some hidden and mysterious (parabolic?) quality which Pilate points to.

> I dreamed I met a Galilean
> A most amazing man
> He had that look you very rarely find
> The haunting hunted kind.

The 'Christology' emergent here is of a piece, I believe, with parabolic indirection: there is no kerygma about Jesus, no Superstar Christology, only a hidden, mysterious, indirect pointing through the familiar events of this very human life to the unfamiliar: 'he's just a man' but 'he scares me so.'

Juxtaposition also operates with individual words and phrases: plays are made on words, as in the slight rephrasing of the words of institution, giving new significance to the old words. The text is extraordinarily biblical; that is, the actual words, with a slight twist or a new setting supplied, are used and the shock of the new twist or context sparks a new perception: 'myrrh for your hot forehead oh then you'll feel fine'; 'If your slate is clean – then you can throw stones'; 'change my water into wine'; 'If every tongue was still the noise would still continue / The rocks and stones themselves would start to sing.' The impious pop culture phrases – 'Jesus is cool,' 'he's top of the poll' – supply the shock ingredient to the perception, for piety is so heavy that nothing less than impiety allows us to *see* the man in the midst of 'Mr Wonderful Christ.' The double entendre, which is another way of describing juxtaposed metaphor used in relation to individual words and phrases, is an important and highly complex feature of *Jesus Christ Superstar* and another way, I believe, in which the parabolic mode is followed.

A final set of juxtapositions is focused on contemporary events: racial strife, poverty, the press, political power, Jesus mania, and money are among the issues dealt with. And this is handled very adroitly: the story of Jesus is taken as the familiar partner in the metaphor while our contemporary situation is taken as the unknown. That is to say, the concrete situation is the narrative before us and we are invited to associate it with our own time. Judas says to Jesus: 'Listen Jesus do you care for your race? Don't you see we must keep in our place?' Both situations are illuminated by the association, though only obliquely and in terms of the entire passion narrative and its resolution. The power motif is a strong one throughout the opera, nicely juxtaposed with the Lord's Prayer by Simon Zealotes:

> You will rise to a greater power
> We will win ourselves a home
> You'll get the power and the glory
> For ever and ever and ever
> Amen! Amen!

Perhaps the finest set of comments on contemporary events through juxtaposition is the temple scene: 'Roll on up – for my price is down / Come on in – for the best in town / Take your pick of the finest wine / Lay your bets on this bird of mine.'

The interesting thing about this opera is that its ethos is fatalistic (Jesus: 'Everything is fixed and you can't change it') and it would therefore be easy to call it anti-Christian and dismiss it. It is frequently remarked in this connection that no resurrection is appended (though Mark does not have one either). But Christian discrimination ought to operate on another level here; it ought to applaud the metaphorical adroitness in giving a new context for the passion story, a context which provides for disbelieving contemporary human beings a genuinely 'secular' experience of the narrative, and one which is in continuity with the parabolic way of hiddenness and mystery.

The humor, irreverence, ambiguity, and irony that are evident in *Jesus Christ Superstar* are also ingredient in Corita Kent's *Footnotes and Headlines: A Play-Pray Book*, a fascinating exercise in metaphorical power which relies on juxtaposition. The supposition is that all the words we need to make the Christian tradition meaningful are lying in wait around us, in ads, in clichés, in common talk.

> we give new life to these words and phrases
> and they give new life to our old stories
> for twenty centuries we have been learning the
>   stories

                    memorizing the script
so we can easily recognize reflections and unconscious
                              allusions to them
        in almost any set of words
            we can lift them out or use them where they
                                          are[17]

        to create is to relate
    we trust in the artist in everybody
        to make his own connections
            his own juxtapositions

    it seems that perhaps there is nothing unholy
                              nothing unrelated

        and that as we fit things together
            synthesize rather than analyze

        we might be coming closer to god's view
            from which all must somehow fit together[18]

The book is intended as an exercise in metaphoric re-creation: a do-it-yourself kit. Each page is a collage of words from ads, comment, color, single letters, pictures – all of which can be put together, juxtaposed, in different ways, though of course delimited and directed by the choice on the pages. The exercise is intended to help people to see the familiar in new contexts, by juxtaposing the ordinary familiar meanings with novel associations: thus Camel filters are juxtaposed with the rich man who wanted to get into the kingdom of heaven, and the ad reads: 'This is the one to try.'

        in trying to get hold of things mysterious
            we try to invent something definite
        and mystery can never be defined
            or must always be redefined
                              or better yet
                    come at newly and indirectly
            through stories and things around us

                thru parables and food[19]

Corita Kent says quite explicitly here what I have been attempting to suggest throughout this essay. Popular Christian literary culture offers an interesting insistence here with its wry, ironical, ambiguous association through juxtaposition. It is parabolic – hidden, understated, secular, irreverent – and while it is only partially successful (it is, after all, much harder to carry off than associative sacramentalism) it is a genuine biblical tradition. If associations, transferences, are made too obviously and openly in a time of disbelief, the result will be sentimental and dishonest. Associations need to be radical – verging on juxtaposition – so that sufficient 'space' is allowed the disbeliever. Juxtaposition may be as far as we can go today.

If theologians were to turn to the poetry – both ancient and modern – we have looked at as a source for their reflection, we might speculate on the kind of theology which would emerge. It would not be mystical, religious, didactic, discursive, or explanatory. It would be sensuous, secular, suggestive, personal, participatory. It would not abjure ambiguity or fear irreverence or humor. It would realize that there is no 'direct' way to talk about God, whether the objective route of Barth with his penchant for biblical language or the subjective route of Bultmann with his reliance on existentialist language. It would, with Elizabeth Sewell, realize that all our talk, including talk about God, is 'anthropomorphic' and not be afraid of such indirection and limitation. It would, perhaps, learn two things from poetic metaphor – to associate when possible ('I caught this morning morning's minion') and to juxtapose when necessary ('They hung him in Jerusalem / And in Hiroshima') – and to be sensitive enough to know the difference.

To understand the way metaphor works is most helpful to theologians in *educating their sensibilities*. It will not write their theology for them and it need not reduce them to silence if they are not themselves poets, but it can make them better able to distinguish between words that are dead and those that are alive. It can make them extremely cautious of a 'high,' open, traditional vocabulary, of words that are simply clichés; it can make them responsive to all kinds of new and undreamt of associations and juxtapositions in ordinary language, eager to use as 'low,' hidden, and contemporary a vocabulary as they believe is illuminating of that other low, hidden, and contemporary story of long ago: the story of Jesus of Nazareth.

If the basic task of theology is to help locate new contexts in which the word of God can be encountered, then theologians have much to learn from the way Christian poets, both ancient and modern, have created such contexts.

Non-Christian Poetry

Perhaps theologians have as much to learn from some non-Christian poets. Christian poetry is practically nonexistent in our time, but good poets of whatever religious persuasion are a source for learning the way metaphor works to create insight. Theirs is always the lowly, parabolic way. Poets can only create their worlds through words referring to experience, and if they care about defining their worlds, their visions, precisely (and all good poetry is precise), they will use every device in their imaginative powers to crack, break, combine, and shuffle words, our worldly words, to their purposes. Unlike mystics, who can abide in silence, in awe before the mystery of it all and hence feel at one with the world and be satisfied with the feeling, poets want to communicate their feelings, or at least define them more precisely to themselves. This means using words, every-day words, that refer to everyday experience in a novel way; it means metaphor. It means speaking of 'camels of the spirit,' 'hurricanes of streets,' 'mad yaks,' 'fat pontiffs of Kindness,' 'false windmills,' and so on. If poets want to convey cosmic oneness with it all, they still have to do so through images, metaphors, symbols – words taken from the world. They cannot talk in abstractions; they find themselves talking about hurricanes, camels, windmills, and so forth. They find themselves affirming the world though it may be only the back-handed compliment that, as poets, they are bound hand and foot to the particular, to the smells and sounds, sights and hurts that surround them.

This is to say, so far, only that *good* poets can teach those concerned with intermediary theological reflection a great deal about how to form new contexts for old truths. But there is more that can be said about *some* contemporary poets, at any rate. It is not simply that poets must work with ordinary words to say their new thing, but some poets are what Paul Van Buren calls 'strange ones' for whom the ordinary things of life strike them as wonderful: 'the decisive point to be made is that some men are *struck* by the ordinary, whereas most find it only ordinary.' He goes on to say that the duality here is not the old duality between time and eternity, man and God, but 'the duality of the ordinary seen as ordinary and the ordinary seen as extraordinary.'[20] One might say that the 'strange ones' are 'anonymous Christians' who have internalized the sense of the illuminated commonplace from Christianity. But it is also a part of poetic insight per se, and all good poets have it to a certain extent. There are, however, some contemporary poets who seem, more than others, to be 'strange ones'; for instance, Denise Levertov, Gary Snyder, Paul Blackburn, Charles Olson, James Dickey, Robert Penn Warren, Richard Wilbur. As Paul Lacey says of the Hasidic tradition out of which Denise Levertov comes and which is reflected in her work: 'One *puts off* the habitual but does not repudiate it; when the habitual is seen afresh, it testifies to the holy.'[21] Or as the same critic says of her poem, 'Illustrious Ancestors,' 'what strikes us first is that the miraculous itself is being treated matter-of-factly.'[22]

> The Rav
> of Northern White Russia declined,
> in his youth, to learn the
> language of birds, because
> the extraneous did not interest him; nevertheless
> when he grew old it was found
> he understood them anyway, having
> listened well, and as it is said, 'prayed
>   with the bench and the floor.' He used
> what was at hand – as did
> Angel Jones of Mold, whose meditations
> were sewn into coats and britches.
>   Well, I would like to make,
> thinking some line still taut between me and them,
> poems direct as what the birds said,
> hard as a floor, sound as a bench,
> mysterious as the silence when the tailor
> would pause with his needle in the air.[23]

The ancestors use 'what was at hand,' the ordinary is the bearer of the miraculous – meditations are sewn into britches, the strange language of the birds is learned simply by having listened well. The author wishes she too might deal in mystery with the directness, hardness, and soundness of what is at hand.

This is the parabolic form – the hidden way of locating the mystery of the universe within the ordinary and the mundane. All good poets practice it to some extent, but the 'strange ones' are cousins to Christians, helping us to see, where there is nothing to see, the presence of transcendent mystery. The theologian concerned with creating new contexts for the ordinary has a peculiar debt to such poets for they, more sometimes than Christian poets, see where others see nothing.

6

The Story:
Coming to Belief

Poetry, Christian poetry, is the most precise and direct metaphorical tradition, creating new contexts for images and symbols of the Christian tradition. One of the reasons that Christian poetry may be so rare in our time is that its direct approach, metaphorical transformation of traditional Christian language, is very difficult indeed in a time of disbelief. Eliot, our latest great Christian poet, avoids Christian language for the most part, seeking, as in the *Four Quartets*, for another language as the objective correlative of his religious experience. As we saw in the last chapter, popular poetry juxtaposes Christian language with contemporary analogues and contrasts and does thereby achieve a kind of ironic distance from that language; but direct contact with traditional language and symbols – what Donne, Herbert, and Hopkins achieved – is not easy, if it is even possible, in our time.

Other genres provide other possibilities: the story and the confession, for instance. The story is a form very close indeed to our primary form, the parable, and its importance for Christianity can scarcely be overstated, as Amos Wilder eloquently insists.

When the Christian in any time or place confesses his faith, his confession turns into a narrative. When the Christian observes Christmas or Easter, in either case it is with reference to a story of things that happened.

It is through the Christian story that God speaks, and all heaven and earth come into it. God is an active and purposeful God and his action with and for men has a beginning, a middle and an end like any good story. The life of a Christian is not a dream

shot through with visions and illuminations, but a pilgrimage, a
race, in short, a history.[1]

The 'history,' whether fictional or real, whether told as a story
or a confession, does not have the precision and purity of poetic
'perspectival individuality.' We find ourselves within the story, even
more than with poetry – or at least in a different way – in the
realm of indirection.* The indirection of poetry is the indirection
of discrete metaphor; the indirection of story is the indirection of
parable as extended metaphor. The parable, as we saw, appears to
be entirely underground except for the cracks in the surface, the
stretching of reality, which allows us to see the new and unfamiliar
context for life, unmerited love. The parabolic story may be, then,
the indirect genre par excellence. But much more will have to be
said to make that statement defensible.

Wilder provides us with some clues. His analysis of story in the
New Testament focuses on the *individual* and on *action.*

> We see, then, that one of the earliest and most important rhetori-
> cal forms in the Church was the story. This is theoretically
> significant. The new movement of the Gospel was not to be
> identified with a new teaching or a new experience but with an
> action and therefore a history. The revelation was in an historical
> drama. The narrative mode inevitably imposed itself as the
> believers rehearsed the saving action, including particular scenes
> of it that played themselves out in the market-place or the
> Temple-court, at a dinner with guests or in a synagogue. The
> locus of the new faith was in concrete human relationships and
> encounters.[2]

The gospel was identified not with a teaching or a 'religious' experience but with an action or history played out in the particular
stories of individuals. The stress on action over against teaching

---

* Or as Stephen Crites says about necessary indirection when dealing with the depths
of human truth, 'Honest men try to tell the truth, but in order to do so they are
obliged, like liars, to tell stories. . . .Stories have been told, and told with imagination,
in the serious attempt to speak the truth that concerns human life most deeply'
('Myth, Story, History,' *Parable, Myth and Language*, ed. Tony Stoneburner [Cam-
bridge: Church Society for College Work, 1968], p. 70).

(the kerygmatic tradition) and religious experience (the mystical tradition) is significant, for it ties in directly with the way of the parables. Or rather we might say, the stress is on experience and belief only *in action*, that is, on the experience of *coming* to belief, the *action* the individual takes in response to an action on his or her behalf by God. The stress on the individual likewise relates story directly to parable, for in each of Jesus' parables it is the life of an individual that is at stake.

The peculiar action of the individual which is at stake is, however, crucial and demands our attention. For, as I suggested above, it is not primarily his or her belief or religious experience that is at the forefront of such parables as the Wedding Feast, the Prodigal Son, the Laborers of the Vineyard, or such stories as those of Peter in the courtyard or Simon of Cyrene, but their lifestyle, or their belief and experience as lived, belief incarnated. One of the interesting things about the men and women in the Scriptural stories is that they appear to be caught in *characteristic* action, at that moment in their lives when they are most themselves, when they reveal themselves most precisely and definitively. Whether it is Abraham sacrificing Isaac, the younger son deciding to return home, the wedding guests refusing the invitation, or Peter denying acquaintance with Jesus, each person appears to be, as Auerbach says of Shakespeare's tragic heroes, 'ripe.'[3]

It is not intellectual belief or momentary experience that is revealed in these stories, but the style of life or belief chosen through a myriad of decisions and now come to a head that is revealed. They are, in other words, *real* individuals, fraught with all the amgibuity, complexity, and richness of those who possess real histories. Sometimes the clue to the reality of their individuality is given only by a phrase – a widow, a younger son; sometimes we see the ligaments and joints of the history, as in Peter's case. But in both instances we know that the parables and stories are being told about timeful individuals. Moreover, they were told to real individuals with equally dense histories – to a man 'desiring to justify himself,' chief priests and Pharisees, a rich man, and so on.

To say that the parables are about the action of individuals and are told to other individuals is not to reduce the gospel to solipsistic ethics. That is what Bultmann comes close to doing, but there is little warrant in the parables for that direction. On the contrary, the story form, because it is concerned with individuals in action, demands just the opposite. Stories always project a 'world,' and, in contrast to lyric poetry, a very public world. The sort of action we find in the parables, for instance, is always decisions in regard to other people – fathers and sons, masters and servants, husbands and wives, citizens and rulers.* Moreover, to say that the parables are told to other individuals does not imply that they are didactic or moralistic. Stories, unlike poetry, are directed outward; the story is a public genre, inviting participation, empathy, identification. The parables are, I have tried to show, extended metaphors, and as such provide insight, but not in a way that can by any stretch of the term be called didactic. If the listener or reader 'learns' what the parable has to 'teach' him or her, it is more like a shock to the nervous system than it is like a piece of information to be stored in the head.

All of this is to say that to see the story as conveying an experience of believing or 'belief in action' is to see it as very close indeed to the parable form, for, as we noted in our comments on the parable of the Wedding Feast, the implied question was, On what logic – that of merit or of grace – do you actually live your life? The question is neither 'religious' nor 'open'; it is a secular question having to do with the social, complex, ambiguous quality of actual human lives. The 'religious' questions are there in the parable of the Wedding Feast – the identity of the king and the relation of Jesus to the parable – but they are given only in 'soft focus.' What we are reaching for is a way of saying that the lowly, contemporary 'way' of the parable is also our way today, not only because it is probably the only way possible for us but because it is *a* if not *the* way of the New Testament as shown in the stories and the parables.†

---

* Stephen Crites' remark on the most physical mark of human individuality, the face, as formed through encounter is a lovely comment on this point. 'A face is in large measure formed by those common and uncommon human transactions which are the substance of history. For people live their lives vis-à-vis. That is perhaps a consequence of their ungainly, gravity-defying posture. Standing upright, they face out toward the horizon, not toward the ground, and so are brought face to face with one another. Words and looks pass between them. When a man is addressed in look or word it is a whole face that addresses him, and his whole face shapes itself in reply. Over the years his face bears the marks of these exchanges and of his personal character that has ripened through them' ('Myth, Story, History,' p. 66).

† There is much that counters this bold assertion, which for someone who is not a New Testament scholar must remain at the most an opinion and at the least a hope. However, the mounting interest in and importance of parable and story in the New

As I mentioned in Chapter 2, the novel owes its central concern with the development of character through temporal decision to biblical stories and preeminently to the story of Jesus, for if, as Erich Auerbach says, God was somehow with Jesus of Nazareth struggling with time and limitation, then human history must be the realm of the truly significant. And Amos Wilder says, 'sometimes one is tempted to think that there is only one story in the world summed up in the formula of "lost and found," and that all the stories long and short in the New Testament or the Bible itself are variations on this theme.'[4] Much the same can be said of the Western novel, not because the majority of the heroes of novels are 'found' (neither are they in the New Testament parables), but because the lost-found struggle, the pattern of the individual in search of his or her real identity is *the* pattern in so many of our novels. Auerbach notes that Dante epitomizes this dramatic notion of salvation which is ingredient both to Christianity and to the novel.

Dante was the first to configure what classical antiquity had configured very differently and the Middle Ages not at all: man, not as remote legendary hero, not as an abstract or anecdotal representative of an ethical type, but man as we know him in his living historical reality, the concrete individual in his unity and wholeness; and in that he has been followed by all subsequent portrayers of man, regardless of whether they treated a historical or a mythical or a religious subject, for after Dante myth and legend also became history.

Man alone, but man in every case regardless of his earthly situation, is and must be a dramatic hero.[5]

The two notes of individuality defined in a social world and action or embodied belief, which we saw are characteristic of Scrip-

---

Testament in the work of a wide variety of New Testament scholars is my evidence for taking this position. Bultmann is basically opposed to it, as are doctrinal theologies of the more open and metaphysical sort, but much traditional theology – Pauline, Augustinian, Lutheran, Calvinistic, Barthian – has significant similarities to it. It has been an important strand in Christian theology and my modest effort is merely to highlight it by looking at some of its clearest manifestations in literary genres of Western Christianity.

tural stories, are also, according to Auerbach, the central qualities of the Western literary tradition. The focus on individual, dramatic, historical destiny in the Western novel is, I believe, a witness to the parabolic or metaphorical tradition, the insistence that the unfamiliar and 'religious' be somehow ingredient in and radically relevant to the mundane contours of complex historical life, that men and women, the human metaphors, be in motion from here to there.

William Lynch says it very explicitly in his *Christ and Apollo*: 'what we need is the restoration of a confidence in the fundamental power of the finite and limited concretions of our human life.'[6] He contrasts the symbol of Apollo with Christ, letting Apollo stand for 'a kind of autonomous and facile intellectualism, a Cartesianism, that thinks form can be given to the world by the top of the head alone,' while Christ stands 'for the completely definite,' 'as the model and source of that energy and courage we again need to enter the finite as the only creative and generative source of beauty.'[7] What Lynch objects to is two kinds of imagination, the univocal and the equivocal, the one which flattens out all the density and variety of historical complexity through the imposition of an idea (the allegorical and didactic mentalities) and the other which sees everything as completely diverse and unrelated to anything else (the fideistic and the autonomous mentalities). What Lynch is driving at with his insistence on the *analogical* imagination, which finds *in* the images of limitation 'the path to whatever the self is seeking: to insight, or beauty, or, for that matter, to God,' is directly related to what I have called metaphor as method.

> This path is both narrow and direct; it leads, I believe, straight through our human realities, through our labor, our disappointments, our friends, our game legs, our harvests, our subjection to time. There are no shortcuts to beauty or truth. We must go *through* the finite, the limited, the definite, omitting none of it lest we omit some of the potencies of being-in-the-flesh.[8]

The univocal and equivocal imaginations deny metaphor, deny that any new insight can come *through the ordinary* – the one flattens it to sameness, the other escapes from it – but what Lynch calls the analogical imagination delves *into* the mundane, for it is precisely in and through the complexities of historical, limited existence that insight comes, if it comes at all. This is, of course, to take the mundane story of Jesus with radical seriousness as *the* metaphor of all human movement.

It may seem that we have wandered far from the story as the central tradition and from the novel as a genre for the metaphorical renewal of Christian belief in our time, but I think not, for all that has been said has been an attempt to show the basically parabolic nature of the novel. It has been an attempt to suggest that the Western novel is haunted by the story of Jesus, in the sense that like the hiddenness of God in that human life, the image of human life in the Western novel is one in which human beings grapple with the transcendent through the inexorable limitations of historical existence. Such a parabolic way is in sharp contrast to the unchanging present of mysticism and the timelessness of the 'message,' both of which deny dramatic growth in time. Mystic simultaneity is very evident on the contemporary scene in the complex phenomenon represented by N. O. Brown, Eastern enlightenment, and drug-induced insight; didactic timelessness is still present in our churches and in *Readers' Digest* Christianity, where reliance on 'right belief' or conversion underlies popular notions of Christian faith.

But Scripture, Auerbach, Lynch, and the Western novel say something much harder *and* more joyful, harder in that the literal and the transcendent are not opposed, but neither is their relationship discovered 'in an instant' or with the top of the head; more joyful because, as Lynch says, 'who wants to overcome the literal?'

Who, if he were honest, would not be happier if he knew that beauty and understanding were completely contained within the literal, the plain, the ordinary, completely self-enclosed fact that meets the eyes and ears?[9]

Who, indeed? But only once, Christians believe, has that unity of the literal and the transcendent been accomplished. It is what the saints strive for, what Dante attempted to suggest in the closing lines of the *Divine Comedy*, what, in a lesser way, many of our best novels grope after as well. And it is terribly hard for a novelist to bring off. Many of the most successful metaphorical novels have been of the nether side; that is, evil is easier to embody, it seems, than good. The parabolic mode, insight into evil through metaphoric transformation, is attempted in Conrad's *Heart of Darkness*, Melville's *Benito Cereno* and *Moby Dick*, Kafka's *The Trial* and *The Castle*, Golding's *The Lord of the Flies*, Tolstoy's *The Death of Ivan Illich*, Mann's *Death in Venice*, Hawthorne's *The Scarlet Letter*. The other possibility, the evocation of the transcendent good – grace, beauty, God – through the hard temporal realities of individuals in action is much harder to carry off, as evidenced in Greene's *The Power and the Glory*, Charles Williams' *Descent into Hell*, C. S. Lewis' *Out of the Silent Planet*, Tolstoy's *Resurrection*, and perhaps most poignantly in the dismal failure of most literary attempts to portray the central mystery, the life of Jesus – Kazantzakis' *The Greek Passion*, Faulkner's *A Fable*, or – most dismal of all, historical novels about Jesus (what could be less hidden?) such as Douglas's *The Robe*. And yet others seem to make it, or almost make it: Silone's *Bread and Wine*, Bernanos' *The Diary of a Country Priest*, Tolkien's *The Lord of the Rings*, Flannery O'Connor's *The Violent Bear It Away*, Dostoevsky's *Crime and Punishment* and *The Brothers Karamazov*, Faulkner's *The Sound and the Fury* and *The Bear*.

It seems to me that these latter novels are all illuminated by discussing them in terms very similar to the ones we used to discuss parables: they evoke the graciousness of the transcendent by means of a distortion of the familiar, for the purpose of providing a new and extraordinary context for ordinary experience. The extraordinary, however, is always disciplined to the inexorable limitations of human dramatic growth in time. In other words, their method is by metaphor, moving from the mundane – but never leaving it behind – to the transcendent by 'figuring' it in terms of the human metaphor. A classic example is from *The Brothers Karamazov*: Alyosha's rapture in Book VII, where 'the mystery of the earth was one with the mystery of the stars.'[10] On the face of it the passage is a mystical experience; but the *way* Alyosha got to it was by way of Father Zossima's putrefying body: he had to go through that experience of radical dissociation, accept it and take it with him, an experience fully described in the earlier part of Book VII, in order to come to the insight that 'the silence of earth seemed to melt into the silence of the heavens.' When he threw himself down and embraced the earth, he was embracing as well the stinking body of Father Zossima.

Parabolic Novels

It might be helpful at this point to look more fully at a few novels that have attempted a parabolic portrayal of the story of the human experience of coming to belief. The examples from which we might choose are many; the ones chosen, however, are representative of different strategies, none of which is entirely successful, but several of which are close to the parabolic form.

Alan Paton's *Cry, the Beloved Country* could be described as a 'Protestant' novel; it comes closer than any other novel I know to telling a story of justification by grace through faith.[11] An old priest, Stephen Kumalo, travels to Johannesburg in search of his son Absalom, and discovers that the boy is convicted of the murder of Arthur Jarvis, son of James Jarvis, the chief white landowner of Kumalo's native valley. The story is one of mounting personal agony for the two fathers, Kumalo and the elder Jarvis, as in different ways they search for their sons, Kumalo for the release of Absalom from the murder charge or at least the boy's repentance for his act, and Jarvis for the significance of his son's life which was devoted to the improvement of the lot of the blacks in South Africa. The personal histories of the fathers and sons are miniatures of the larger black-white confrontation in South Africa, the pattern of social disintegration and the hope for its moral restoration. It is a painful tale, burdened with an inexorable logic of defeat at the hands of a racist society – we 'know' from the beginning that terrible things are in store – but illuminated by another logic, that of grace, by no means so certain, for it operates in secret with persons (Kumalo and the elder Jarvis) whose formation by it is in terms of the gradual and ambiguous growth of actual human development.

Yet *Cry, the Beloved Country* is in some ways a 'message' book, it is within the didactic Christian tradition and not, I believe, in the parabolic tradition at its best. I say this in spite of the fact that in language and tone it is probably the most 'biblical' novel ever written. The novel has a lesson, a moral, to teach, not unlike the lesson of *Uncle Tom's Cabin*, and one doubts whether it would have been written apart from social outrage; it can be taken as propaganda. But one cannot, I think, classify and put down this novel that way, and in any event a propagandistic novel, a novel of social protest, can have considerable aesthetic impact. This one does, and the reason it does, I believe, has to do with the parabolic way in which the message is handled; the message, through various techniques, is rendered indirectly so that the insight gained by the reader is genuinely though not overwhelmingly metaphorical. It is, in any event, not a straightforwardly didactic book.

In the first place, there are no direct statements by the author. Dialogue predominates and many voices, many points of view are heard; such a multitude of voices cannot be unified discursively, and they never are. It is an oral book, not a visual one, so that movement and variety rather than stasis and simplicity are central. Of the thirty-six chapters, only two are straight narrative; the rest are a mingling of lyric and dramatic modes. The complexity and pain of the social theme are *shown*, not preached. The variety of voices is heightened by the different dialogue styles Paton uses: the lyric, almost biblical way he renders the Zulu dialect; the cliché-ridden language of the commercially-oriented, English-speaking community; the chanting rhythms and repetition of the native 'chorus'; the clear, logical, terse style of the educated black priest who helps Kumalo find Absalom; the cynical, humorous tone of chapter 23, a satire on justice.

A second major parabolic device is the complex personal story of the fathers and sons which implicitly carries the larger story, the social story of the black-white confrontation. The personal story is intricate and convincing; it supplies metaphors for the disintegration-restoration pattern, and they serve it well. Mention was made earlier of Amos Wilder's comment that all biblical stories might be understood in terms of the 'lost-found' motif. That is certainly true of this story, which explicitly incorporates the Prodigal Son parable on several levels, not only the relation of the fathers to their lost sons, but Kumalo as an elder brother who hates his younger brother, John, a prodigal. Reminiscences of other painful stories are also recalled in the names 'Absalom' and 'Stephen.' But more important than the mythic dimensions is the agonizing temporal development of the two fathers as they work toward acceptance not only of their sons' deaths but of each other, the murderer's father and the murdered one's father. Paton is too much given to coincidences and neat juxtapositions, and the final restoration – growing intimacy between the fathers, the coming of an agricultural advisor to restore the valley's deteriorating land, the presence of another son in the murdered Jarvis's boy, and the hope of yet another one in the womb of Absalom's wife – seems too good to be true. But parabolic hiddenness is what predominates, I believe, in the stories of the fathers and sons, and because Paton has shown the reader through dramatic personal growth the pattern of disintegration and restoration, he has created an extended metaphor of the experience of coming to belief in the workings of the gracious transcendent in both personal and social realities.

To move from Paton's novel to works by C. S. Lewis and Charles Williams is to move to another universe. If Paton's novel verges on being a message, Lewis' and Williams' novels come close to being allegories. Both the message and the allegory have been sturdy traditions in Christian literature and, as Lynch suggested in his comments on the univocal imagination, they share the characteristic of tending to flatten out the complexities of historical life for the sake of the 'idea.' We noted that tendency in Paton's too-neat coincidences and restoration, but it is far more pronounced, in very different ways, in Lewis and Williams. These novelists are more complex than Paton: reading Paton is like reading 'Bible stories'; reading Lewis and Williams is like reading medieval theology. No attempt will be made here to 'do them justice'; the literature on the complexity of their romantic religion, sacramentalism, favorite theological doctrines, literary techniques, and the like is vast, and it is not our main concern. I am concerned, rather, with the parabolic qualities of their novels as illustrations for my thesis that the experience of coming to belief is a story and novels which tell that story are a source for theological reflection.

In that respect Lewis and Williams do not come off very well. To put it simply, most of their work is high-level illustration of supernatural truth, not stories of people on the move toward belief. Lewis' most successful novel, I believe, is the first part of his science-fiction trilogy, *Out of the Silent Planet*, in which a Cambridge don named Ransom is kidnapped by two diabolical characters, the scientist Weston and the entrepreneur Devine, and transported via rocket ship as a sacrificial victim to the inhabitants of another planet called Malacandra (Mars).[12] The reason this novel is successful is that it is the least allegorical of his works; there are few one-to-one relations between the characters and events of the novel and some outside structure or pattern of ideas. Another way to say this is that the novel is only implicitly Christian, or that it is mythopoeic; it envisions another world, a world before the fall – created goodness, if you will – which has an integrity in its own right. What the reader, or at least this reader, retains of the novel is not a pattern of Christian belief but descriptions of the three kinds of rational creatures who inhabit the planet and of the fantastic shapes and smells and pastel colors of the beautiful land.

> A mass of something purple, so huge that he took it for a heather-covered mountain, was his first impression: on the other side, beyond the larger water, there was something of the same kind. But there, he could see the top of it. Beyond were strange upright shapes of whitish green: too jagged and irregular for buildings, too thin and steep for mountains. Beyond and above these again was the rose-coloured cloud-like mass. It might really be a cloud, but it was very solid-looking. . . .

> It looked like the top of a gigantic red cauliflower – or like a huge bowl of red soapsuds – and it was exquisitely beautiful in tint and shape.[13]

Descriptions such as this one convey a dream-like quality, an Eden quality, entirely appropriate to such an innocent world; the reader gains a sense of what such a world must feel like, not what it means. Dreaming innocence is not, however, human life, and when Lewis contrasts Malacandra and 'the silent planet' (earth), his low estimate of human life becomes evident: when Ransom acknowledges to one of the rational creatures that the speck through the telescope is his planet, 'It was the bleakest moment in all his travels.' Because Lewis has kept the action in this novel on the supernatural level, in the nontemporal, a-historical Eden, he can affirm life here; but the contrast between Malacandra and earth is such that human life is seen as brutal and brutish.

Charles Williams' early novel, *The Place of the Lion*, is so blatantly supernatural and allegorical that it will serve a useful role in analyzing the type.[14] This little novel tells of curious happenings in a small contemporary English village: ordinary animals and people, it seems, are suddenly turning into extraordinary creatures, into the invisible, supernatural ideas or forms of which our natural examples are but faint images.

'He believes – and I believe it too,' Mr. Foster said, 'that this world is created, and all men and women are created by the entrance of certain great principles into aboriginal matters. We call them by cold names; wisdom and courage and beauty and strength and so on, but actually they are very great and mighty Powers. . . .Our knowledge will more and more be a knowledge of that and not of this – more and more everything will be received into its original, animals, vegetables, all the world but those individual results of interior Powers which are men.'[15]

'Men' eventually go the way of the animals and vegetables, however, as the hero becomes Adam. It is heavily allegorical and the reader must work constantly to get the metaphysics straight, which is obviously a more important job than attending to the characters, who, after all, are only images and substitutable. The real world is the supernatural world: the natural proceeds from it and is secondary to it. What this amounts to from a literary perspective is seeing the story as merely a frame and the characters as useful mediums for dramatizing the ideology. It is important to note that Williams' variety of sacramentalism is oriented to nature, not to human beings; to vision, not to hearing; to space, not to time; and magic is the key to transformation, not dramatic growth. In magic anything might turn into anything else in the twinkling of an eye before one's face; but such nature-oriented, visual, spatial, magical imagery has little if anything to do with human transformation. Nor does it have anything to do with the form that reflects the way of human transformation – the parabolic, hidden way that works *through* the complexities and the sharp angles of time and glimpses the gracious transcendent only in the density of the ordinary. Williams' sacramentalism is in the head – if one gets the pattern, one has gotten the main thing; once Pauline, in *Descent into Hell*, understands the notion of co-inherence, the mutual sharing of burdens, her struggle is largely over. Williams has written that 'the world exists for the Incarnation' rather than the Incarnation for the world';[16] a statement like this puts the operation strictly from the top down, and that is precisely the problem with intellectual sacramentalism. All sorts of transformations can occur in the mind and to things, but human transformation is parabolic, metaphorical transformation – it is historical, and complex.

When we turn to more successful examples of parabolic novels, there are many from which we might choose, as was suggested earlier. Our choice of two – J. R. R. Tolkien's *The Lord of the Rings* and Flannery O'Connor's *The Violent Bear It Away* – is therefore somewhat arbitrary, but not entirely, for so much has been written about such novels as *The Brothers Karamazov* and *The Sound and the Fury*, and the stories of Alyosha and Dilsey are such perfect illustrations of the parabolic way, that they are almost too easy. Tolkien and O'Connor offer more of a challenge, for the initial impact of reading either of these authors may well be exactly the opposite of appreciating the metaphorical potential of their works. Tolkien's fantasy of little people and strange creatures, of evil powers and gracious rescues seems anything but parabolic; O'Connor's stories of Jesus-haunted heroes constantly talking about the bread of life and 'the sweat and stink of the cross' hardly seem to be more likely candidates. But I think both are strangely and marvelously parabolic.

Tolkien in *The Lord of the Rings* creates a 'Secondary World' complete in itself, related to the 'Primary World' as fantasy is related to imagination, that is, 'secondarily.'[17] Unlike Lewis and Williams, he offers no suggestion of supernature-nature, superior-inferior; the world created by fantasy is a world unto itself, having secondary relations with the real world which, however, are nowhere spelled out. What *is* created is a world believable on its own terms, so that the reader need exercise no suspension of disbelief, experience no conflict with science, no dislocation through the necessity of discovering what characters and events 'mean.' They do not mean anything other than who they are and what happens, for the story is, I believe, a parable. To be sure, the cracks in the realistic surface, the surrealism, are far greater than in parables in the 'Primary World,' but the story is still parabolic, for the transcendent unfamiliar, both good and evil, operative in this tale works within the givens of this world. The peculiar way this parabolic action takes place in *The Lord of the Rings* is, however, more mythic than human, and what I mean by this is that in contrast to subjective, dramatic human growth (such as O'Connor depicts in Francis Tarwater), the movement in Tolkien's trilogy is more external, more the grace of power than of persuasion. But this is possible and right in a fantasy world, for the givens of this world are not highly complex beings; the focus is not on human transformation but on the struggle of good and evil forces in the world, a struggle of mythic proportions, and it can be resolved mythically.

This is not to say that the novels are allegories, for they are not: the imagery is largely unassigned. Nor is it to say that the struggle is a-historical, that it takes place 'above' the characters or uses them; it is not a supernatural struggle. It is a deeply historical struggle in the world of the Hobbits, Dwarves, Ents, Orcs, Sauron, and the wizards; given this kind of world, the mythic struggle of good and evil is the parabolic way to portray it.

Another way to put this is to say that in order to see this tale as parabolic one must allow Tolkien's world to be 'the world,' and, as many have discovered, this is not hard to do. One reason may be the extraordinarily temporal character of Middle-earth. It is not, like Lewis' and Williams' worlds, spatial, a world which one sees with one's mind but which could in an instant vanish. Rather it is, on its own terms, deeply, densely historical, stretching back for eons (concerning which Tolkien appends one hundred pages of genealogies and other data) and covering within the story so many incidents, so much detail, that one could not possibly 'see' it or hold it in one's mind; one can only feel it, grasp it with the imagination. Having gotten in on and accepted this world, the operations of good and evil are entirely appropriate. It is the way of *this* world.

But the trilogy is, because of this peculiar 'mythic' nature, metaphorical in yet a more precise way. For what the mythic pattern, the heightened renditions of good and evil – the Gandalf rescuers and the Sauron evil lords – allow for is what Tolkien elsewhere has called 'recovery,' seeing things as we were meant to see them. Writing of Tolkien's notion of 'recovery,' a recent commentator says,

All things become blurred by familiarity; we come to possess them, to use them, to see them only in relation to ourselves. In so doing we lose sight of what the things themselves really are *qua* things – and 'things' here includes people, objects, ideas, moral codes, literally everything. *Recovery* is recovery of perspective. . . .

We re-discover the meaning of heroism and friendship as we see the two hobbits clawing their way up Mount Doom; we see again the endless evil of greed and egotism in Gollum, stunted and ingrown out of moral shape by years of lust for the ring; we recognize again the essential anguish of seeing beautiful and frail things – innocence, early love, children – passing away as we read of the Lady Galadriel and the elves making the inevitable journey to the West.[18]

The way to the recovery of perception is accomplished here through the *heightening* of things, making the familiar more alive, more potent, more splendid than it is in the 'Primary World.' The unfamiliar, the sight of things in their singularity, is accomplished by the deformation of the familiar in the direction of the larger than life: this is the mythic way to stretch reality, to open the cracks into it.

But it is not an entirely satisfactory way for human beings, for, as I mentioned earlier, the action of the transcendent is largely external, and little reformation through moral choice and persuasive grace takes place. Frodo, the hobbit who over these three novels journeys with a magic ring whose evil powers must be destroyed to save Middle-earth, refuses at the last moment to part with the ring. He puts it on his finger, and an overriding if somewhat ambiguous grace in the figure of the treacherous Gollum comes to the rescue by biting off Frodo's ring finger and going down with the ring into the chasm at the Mount of Dom.

Flannery O'Connor's novel *The Violent Bear It Away* does suggest a more satisfactory relation for human beings between the ordinary and the transcendent though it is, on the face of it, a very strange one indeed.[19] Her novel is about a fourteen-year-old boy, Francis Tarwater, who, after the death of his great-uncle, a self-proclaimed prophet, goes to his uncle Rayber in order to fulfill the Lord's 'call' that he, Tarwater, baptize Rayber's young idiot son. Tarwater fights the call and comes to fulfill it only by way of the tortuous route of slowly realizing the shallowness of Rayber's rationalistic secularism and his own deep allegiance to and need for 'the bread of life.' It is a richly complex, many-layered novel, abounding in biblical and traditionally religious language and in discrete metaphors which, by placing that language in new contexts, renews it.

Flannery O'Connor was a devout Catholic, deeply influenced by Southern fundamentalism, a woman of enormous passion, wit, and commitment, with a religious view of life so overwhelming that she can be compared only to Pascal, Kierkegaard, and Dostoevsky – and perhaps to Barth. In commenting on her own work, she made the following very interesting statement.

> I see from the standpoint of Christian orthodoxy. This means that for me the meaning of life is centered in our Redemption by Christ and that what I see in the world I see in its relation to that. I don't think that this is a position that can be taken half-way or one that is particularly easy in these times to make transparent in fiction.[20]

Her Catholicism is in many ways old-style, pre-Vatican II. Good and evil, the battle, often violent, of God and the devil for the individual soul is central. She is concerned not with the salvation of the world in social or economic terms – no agricultural experts here! – but the baptism of idiots. Tarwater's first and despised duty as a fledgling prophet is to baptize the idiot boy: this counts in her scheme of things. This is a sort of religiosity that it is difficult for modern, secular people to understand and appreciate; she goes against the grain not only of the more obvious kind of rationalistic secularism embodied in Rayber but against all of the best in liberal Christianity, whether Catholic or Protestant. Evil is pervasive, substantial in her work, in a way reminiscent of Dostoevsky. Raskolnikov in *Crime and Punishment* 'had to' commit murder to start on the road to redemption. Violence, evil, battle, passion – the extremes – are integral to her vision. God and Christ *fight* for man's soul. Tarwater (tar: sin; water: baptism) is Everyman, another Prodigal Son, on the universal journey from evil to salvation. But unlike the morality plays which this pattern suggests, O'Connor's novel is not an allegory.

   She manages to deal with this whole supernatural belief package through what she calls embodying 'mystery through manners' and what I would call creating a parable or an extended metaphor. 'It is the business of fiction to embody mystery through manners and mystery is a great embarrassment to the modern mind.'[21]

   This brings us to the heart of O'Connor's extraordinary achievement, and it brings us also to the question of her art as parabolical and metaphorical. The best way to approach this question is through what she calls prophetic vision, for it is both her central aesthetic insight and the theme as well as the achievement of her novels, particularly of *The Violent Bear It Away*.

> Prophecy, which is dependent on the imaginative and not the moral faculty, need not be a matter of predicting the future. The prophet is a realist of distances, and it is this kind of realism that goes into great novels. It is the realism which does not hesitate to distort appearances in order to show a hidden truth.[22]

The prophet is a 'realist of distances,' one who sees things with their extensions of meaning and thus sees far things close up. It is a paradoxical double vision: simultaneously keeping in focus the universal implications of a particular present as well as the potential particularization of the universal and eternal. It is, for example, Tarwater learning of his own history – his whore mother and his birth at the scene of a wreck – *in the context* of the history of Adam and the Second Coming; it is in the remark by the Negro hand on old Tarwater: 'He was deep in this life, he was deep in Jesus' misery'; it is Bishop, the idiot, whose fish eyes are the center of that 'extension' into unreasonable, absurd love for both Tarwater and Rayber. Prophetic vision of this sort – in other words, metaphor, the linking within one image of the 'this here' with the 'that there,' the distortion of appearances 'in order to show a hidden truth' – is everywhere in this novel. It is its *movement* in the deepest sense for it is precisely seeing near things with their extensions of meaning and seeing far things close up which allows Tarwater to reject Rayber's secularism and to embrace the call of the Lord. It is also, of course, what we have called the metaphorical *method*, taking the human in all its particularity and mundanity as one partner in associations to move beyond the human – but in such a way that that human is never left behind.

This metaphorical vision is what separates O'Connor from both fundamentalism, with its literalism, and from Barth, with his avoidance, if not fear, of the sensuous, temporal, and concrete. She is doctrinal, but her doctrine is thoroughly embodied. At the same time one says that *The Violent Bear It Away* is a religious novel with a vengeance, and that the supernatural appears to be everywhere evident in it, one must also say that it is thoroughly parabolic – the supernatural never obtrudes. The supernatural, embodied in the manners of Southern fundamentalism, is not another world impinging on and depreciating this world. The supernaturalism is ingredient in the story; the manners convey the mystery, a mystery which is worked into the story, *is* the story, by means of the manners. Thus Tarwater's pilgrimage, within the givens of this novel, its 'world,' is a thoroughly historical and mundane one: he journeys out of 'the stinking shadow of Jesus,' back into it again through hard personal decisions and actions, not through visions or miracles. There is nothing miraculous or supernatural about the action of this novel; it is thoroughly parabolic. To be sure, the distances are collapsed and events are stretched, but this is of the nature of parable and metaphor; the ability to collapse and stretch is the province of the imagination and of its offspring, metaphor.

Theology and Story

Why does everyone love a good story and how is story related to theological reflection? The answers to these two questions are, I believe, related. We all love a good story because of the basic narrative quality of human experience*; in a sense, any story is about ourselves, and a good story is *good* precisely because somehow it rings true to human life. Human life is not marked by instantaneous rapture and easy solutions. Life is tough. That is hardly a novel thought, but it is nonetheless the backbone in a literal sense – the 'structure' – of a good story. We recognize our own pilgrimages from here to there in a good story; we feel its movement in our bones and know that it is 'right.' The imitation theory of the truth of art has at least this on its side: in a sense a good story, a true story, is 'true to' the structure of human experience. It is also, of course, a deformation of that experience, the placement of that story in a new context, and it is this that makes for the creativity of art, its novelty, moving us beyond where we are. We love stories, then, because our lives are stories and we recognize in the attempts of others to move, temporally and painfully, our own story. We recognize in the stories of others'

---

* '. . . the formal quality of experience through time is inherently narrative. . . . The self in its concreteness is indivisible, temporal, and whole, as it is revealed to be in the narrative quality of its experience. Neither disembodied minds nor mindless activity can appear in stories. There the self is given whole, as an activity in time' (Stephen Crites, 'The Narrative Quality of Experience,' pp. 291, 309).

experiences of coming to belief our own agonizing journey and we rejoice in the companionship of those on the way.

For the Christian, the story of Jesus is *the* story par excellence. For his story not only is the human struggle of moving toward belief but in some way that story *is* the unification of the mundane and the transcendent. That God should be with us in the story of a human life could be seen as a happy accident, but it makes more sense to see it as God's way of always being with human beings *as they are*, as the concrete, temporal beings who have a beginning and an end – who are, in other words, themselves stories.

What ought theology to make of this? Obviously a great deal. To see belief not as a set of beliefs but as a story, an experience of coming to belief, means that theological reflection ought itself to be shaped by the story, take to itself, both in form and content, the story. Theological reflection of the sort I have in mind would be narrative and concrete, telling stories – after all, even the creeds, those monuments of doctrinal formulation, do this! From the novelist as well as from the stories in Scripture the theologian should take courage to concentrate on the experience of coming to belief, not on the 'beliefs' themselves (the sedimentation of experiences of coming to belief). The latter job, the systematic one, is necessary always, but the more crucial task for our time – the task that will help people to hear the word of God – is the more difficult one of locating, testing, and understanding those stories – artistic, personal, social, and political – which carry experiences of coming to belief. This is, of course, what the story of the people of Israel is to the Jewish theologian, what the story of black oppression is to the black theologian, what the story of the poor is to the third-world theologian.

The story form is of peculiar importance to Christians, but, as Stephen Crites indicates, not to them alone. 'A man's sense of his own identity seems largely determined by the kind of story which he understands himself to have been enacting through the events of his career, the story of his life.'[23] It is basic to *human* experience as such, to one's sense of identity. We learn who we are through the stories we embrace as our own – the story of my life is structured by the larger stories (social, political, mythic) in which I understand my personal story to take place. Moreover, as William Beardslee insists, the story form tells the individual 'where he has come from and where he is going,' since 'by creating its own ordered world, wherein through struggle and action an end is achieved, the story expresses faith in the ultimate reality of order and life.'[24] The gospel story, modeled on the story of Jesus, does this and more – it not only provides an ordered context from the past (as do all sacred stories) but also leads from the past into the future, for the gospel story, strongly eschatalogical, is a story of hope.

The centrality of story to human experience and to Scripture raises a question. There is a good deal of discussion currently about the primary literary genre in the Christian gospel – sermon, story, parable, and so on. I think William Beardslee correctly suggests that perhaps no one form need be pressed as primary in the New Testament or in the history of Christianity, but that there are different ways of bringing faith to expression, and different preferences make for different kinds of theological reflection. For instance, Beardslee maintains that the story with its ordered world (and theology based on the story) expresses faith in order and life.[25] But our time, as Beardslee admits, is not one of narrative order – our novels lack plots, resolutions, and developed characters. If one thinks of some of our most interesting novelists – John Barth, Kurt Vonnegut, Joseph Heller, Günter Grass, Donald Barthelme, or Vladimir Nabokov – one must admit that the ordered world of the story apparently does not seem possible to them. One can, of course, criticize such novelists for failure to speak to our deep need for ordered narratives, but to do so, and then, as is often the case, to prefer as more 'Christian' novelists those who still have plots and developed characters but are often second-rate, is to be false not only to the temper of our age but also, I believe, to the resources of the Christian tradition.

Perhaps it is necessary to admit that the narrative, at least in the grand nineteenth-century tradition of Tolstoy, Austen, and Melville, is not the form for our time. Where first-rate novelists are able to be narrative, as in the case of Doris Lessing, William Faulkner, and Alexander Solzhenitsyn, we should rejoice in their accomplishments, for they provide unusually rich resources for the theologian in understanding what it means, in contemporary terms, to create metaphors of coming (or failing to come) to belief. But when the narrative form lacks integrity, as it seems to for many contemporary novelists, it cannot be insisted upon. It may be that the parable, while itself a story of a certain kind, is a more appropriate genre for our time, for unlike more developed narratives it does not call for the same degree of faith in cosmic or even societal ordering. It is a more skeptical form with regard to such matters, insisting that the gap between the human and the transcendent is closed only through personal risk and decision. It only insists that the secular and the human is the place of God's presence – a presence for the most part hidden under the ordinary events of everyday life. It insists, in other words, on faith, not on an ordered structure built into the nature of things upon which the individual can rely. The parable is the form for a secular people, and it is interesting to note that many of the novelists mentioned earlier have strong parabolic elements in their works.

All this is not to say that the story is not central to Christianity – it is at the center of the tradition, as we have insisted all along. But it seems to me that a particular kind of story, the parabolic story, the kind of story which does not *assume* an ordered world but perceives order only indirectly, intermittently, and beneath the complexities of personal and social chaos, is the kind most pertinent to our times. To admit this is by no means to sell out to cultural relevance, for the parables of Jesus, and Jesus himself as the parable of God, are such stories.

If theological reflection were to model itself on such stories, on parabolic stories, what would it be like? It would, I believe, not fear secularity, hiddenness, ironic distance, and indirection in the experience of coming to belief. It would not insist on open declarations or solid resolutions; it would realize that genuine human experiencing is so complex and intricate that such declarations and resolutions are often not possible and, if insisted upon, not honest. It would learn these things not principally from the 'content' of the stories but from their 'form'; whether a novel is, like O'Connor's, an experience of coming to belief within a recognizably Christian universe, or, like Kurt Vonnegut's *Slaughterhouse-Five*, an experience of deepening despair over the ways of the universe, it would see them both as parabolic stories. Richard R. Niebuhr says that 'believing is not commanded by beliefs. Beliefs come from believing; and believing is generated in experience.'[26] If this is true, then the complexity, hiddenness, and skepticism inherent in human experience of anything cannot be denied, and they can be denied least when the experience in question is that of coming to belief. As H.

Richard Niebuhr says with characteristic eloquence in this passage, they surely ought not to be denied by Christians.

> But now for Christians Jesus Christ appears not only as the symbol of an ethos in which the ultimate response to the inscrutable power in all things is one of trust. He is also the one who accomplishes in them this strange miracle, that he makes them suspicious of their deep suspicion of the Determiner of Destiny. He turns their reasoning around so that they do not begin with the premise of God's indifference but of his affirmation of the creature, so that the *Gestalt* which they bring to their experiences of suffering as well as of joy, of death as well as of life, is the *Gestalt*, the symbolic form, of grace. That so to reason and so to perceive requires a great relearning which is never completed in their lives; that for the most part they do not reason and interpret on the basis of the new premise but on that of the old; that they tend to interpret the action upon them by which they are and by which they cease to be as inimical or indifferent; that they respond therefore for the most part in the manner of an ethics of death, Christians agree. Their true life, man's true life, is still hidden, as Paul says, with Christ in God. That is one of many reasons why they cannot defend themselves or recommend themselves. But the hope of that life of universal responsibility, of citizenship in the country of being itself, of reaction in all reactions to the God of grace, to the grace which is God – that hope is there, and there is rejoicing when the potentiality that has been put into life becomes for some brief moment an actuality. . . . Thus Christians understand themselves and their ethos, or somewhat in this fashion. They cannot boast that they have an excellent way of life for they have little to point to when they boast. They only confess – we were blind in our distrust of being, now we begin to see; we were aliens and alienated in a strange, empty world, now we begin sometimes to feel at home; we were in love with ourselves and all our little cities, now we are falling in love, we think, with being itself, with the city of God, the universal community of which God is the source and governor. And for all this we are indebted to Jesus Christ, in our history, and in that depth of the spirit in which we grope with our theologies and theories of symbols.[27]

Autobiography:
The Unity of Life and Thought

An autobiography is a story, the story of a life, and the best autobiographies are written precisely as a story, that is, as an ordering of events around a central focus. Like a good story, a good autobiography deals with a great unfamiliar, the mystery of the self, in and through the familiar, a multitude of events and circumstances. If the autobiography is true, it points to the self elliptically through these events and circumstances; in other words, a successful autobiography is very similar to a parable. A religious autobiography or confession is similar, except that here the unfamiliar is not the 'interesting' self but the self in relation to God. What shines through indirectly in a confession is God's hand in the intricacies of an actual, historical life. The most parabolic of the confessions are not the mystical, self-absorbed ones – the confessions of the medieval saints and the Puritans – but the ones in which the self is vocationally integrated into the ambiguity and complexity of temporal life. The self's participation in this public world becomes the setting for the parable of God's dealing with a man or woman. To take as examples two modern Christian confessions, Sam Keen's *To a Dancing God* is, on these terms, much less parabolic than is Dorothy Day's *The Long Loneliness*. Keen is mainly absorbed with his own person; Day, by her vocation in the world in relation to God.

The lives of the saints are in many instances such parables (often literally so, because of their legendary elements), which for centuries have provided intimations of the grace of God working in the ordinary, temporal circumstances of particular human lives. There may be little interest in the lives of the saints these days, and when these lives are understood primarily as imitations of the life of Jesus, as direct attempts to do what he did, there is ample reason for turning from them. But not all of the saints attempted direct imitation;

many were struggling, public men and women who took the ordinary contemporaneous way and who made their 'confession' in the world. Where they succeeded, their lives are paradigms of a primary form in Scripture, the parable.

The three levels we have been concerned with in this essay – language, belief, and life-style – are integrated in this third level, for language and belief are here hammered out in a life; the integrity of the new insights one has come to through language and belief are now painfully tested in one's life. Throughout this essay we have not been talking about three things, of course, but about one – about the *parabolic form* of language, belief, and life; but it is here, in life, *in each one's own life*, that everything focuses. Matters are likely to get uncomfortable from now on. It is no longer only a question of poetry and novels, of language and of belief, but of the parabolic possibilities of *my own life*.

No one appears yet to have asked why autobiographies (and indeed all personal documents) are so interesting to read. The reason, in part, may be that the reader semiconsciously reflects on his own life as he reads about another's, and his interest accordingly stems from his own self-love.[1]

We read autobiographies to find out about *ourselves*. The other is a medium, a metaphor, into that desert, *myself*. In autobiographies we see people in what could be called the 'last lecture' stance.[2] It is as if one had but an hour to say what is most important to the speaker – the leisure and pseudo-objectivity are gone. Whatever is communicated must come with immediacy, intimacy, intensity, and involvement. In other words, in the midst of whatever other questions are raised, one always first and foremost raises the question of *oneself*.

One of the most interesting characteristics of our contemporary culture is its intense interest in the self, in autobiography, in life-styles.* There are many levels of this fascination, from the interest of

---

* Fascination with the self is not a twentieth-century phenomenon. The Romantic poets, and particularly a poet such as G. M. Hopkins, were consumed by it. In his *Devotional Writings* Hopkins says, 'I find myself both as man and as myself something most determined and distinctive, at pitch, more distinctive and higher pitched than anything else I see; I find myself with my pleasures and pains, my powers and my experiences, my deserts and guilt, my shame and sense of beauty, my dangers, hopes,

the general population in the TV documentary and the nonfiction novel (Capote's *In Cold Blood*, Styron's *Nat Turner*) to the dedication of many to communes and utopian societies in the search for their true selves. Sociology and psychology (Oscar Lewis, Studs Terkel, Robert Coles, Erik Erikson, Viktor Frankl, R. D. Laing) have adopted the experiential, documentary approach in a search for authenticity; Theodore Roszak mentions that 'for most of the New Left, there has ultimately been no more worth or cogency in any ideology than a person lends it by virtue of his own action; personal commitments, not abstract ideas, are the stuff of politics.'[3] Bonhoeffer, Camus, Malcolm X, Martin Luther King, the Berrigan brothers have been our heroes – people whose lives reflect, sometimes to the death, what they say.

It would appear, then, that the self is the place to begin. But *who* am I?

> The self . . . is infinitely difficult to get at, to encompass, to know how to deal with: it bears no definition; it squirts like mercury away from observation; it is not known except privately and intuitively; it is for each of us, only itself, unlike anything else experienced or experienceable.[4]

Not only is the self elusive, but, to make the matter more complex, the self's projections are the 'world,' our world. What we *know* are the metaphors or projections of the self, the worlds it creates. The relativity of knowledge demands such a perspective. Without assuming an idealistic perspective (the world out there is only what subjects say it is), a moderate Kantianism (and we are all, one way or another, Kantians) insists that in a sense, as James Olney says, all theology, philosophy, physics, and art is autobiography.[5] To put the question the other way, try to imagine the world *without* human beings – a world that is unseen, uninterpreted, silent. What *is* it? We do not know quite how to answer that question. As Hopkins says in his *Journal*, 'What you look hard at seems to look hard at you,' but *our* looking comes first: the self has a priority. In a real sense, what the world *is* is what we say it is and we say it is what *we* are. The world, as Hopkins says, always has 'the taste of me.'

---

fears, and all my fate, more important to myself than anything I see' (as quoted in Olney, *Metaphors of Self*, p. 24).

There is, then, from a number of points of view a priority to the self – epistemologically, existentially, scientifically, artistically. It is hard to deny where modernity has landed us – after Galileo toppled us from the center of the universe, human beings are, curiously, back there again, albeit in a somewhat different guise. In a sense we are 'stuck' with our centrality: we cannot, finally, get outside of ourselves, we cannot jump out of our skins. But what many voices increasingly are saying – from the existentialist tradition to the women's movement – is, 'Why should we want to?' As Olney comments, what we all seek is not happiness or achievement but to be ourselves – to realize the destiny that is me: to create, to recognize, to realize one's own daimon.[6]

We are turned back again, then, as we have been several times during these comments, to the self. But when we start with the self, *what* do we start with? Ignorance, as Socrates reminds us. We know nothing about 'the self,' let alone our own selves. There has always been great suspicion about autobiography: people not only lie outrageously and cover up the 'true' self, but even when they honestly try to uncover it they meet the old onion-peeling problem.

> The moment we want to say *who* somebody is, our very vocabulary leads us astray into saying *what* he is; we get entangled in a description of qualities he necessarily shares with others like him; we begin to describe a type or a 'character' in the old meaning of the word, with the result that his specific uniqueness escapes us. . . .The point is that the manifestation of the 'who' comes to pass in the same manner as the notoriously unreliable manifestations of ancient oracles, which, according to Heraclitus, 'neither reveal nor hide in words, but give manifest signs.'[7]

Yet, as Hannah Arendt insists, there is a solution to the enigma she poses in this quotation, for people *do* reveal who they are in their speech and action, and both are necessary, for without language action would be the movements of robots, and without action speech would disintegrate into abstract passivity.* But together, action and

---

* The relation of action to identity, the *necessity* of specifying the agent of action, is illustrated in the following comment by Arendt: 'Action without a name, a "who" attached to it, is meaningless. . . .The monuments to the "Unknown Soldier" after World War I bear testimony to the then still existing need for glorification, for finding a "who," an identifiable somebody whom four years of mass slaughter should

speech become the 'sign,' the metaphor, disclosing indirectly *who* one is. Hence, as Arendt points out, who somebody is is revealed only in action accompanied by speech, by, in other words, a story or drama. In Greek tragedy, for instance, the universal meanings are revealed by the chorus, 'whereas the intangible identities of the agents in the story, since they escape all generalization and therefore all reification, can be conveyed only through an imitation of their acting.'[8]* The way to the self, as Arendt suggests, goes through indirection, through the story of the self in speech and action as a metaphor or parable of the self. We cannot look at the self directly, for like mercury it squirts away from our sight; but we can evoke the self through a similitude of it, through the metaphor we call autobiography.

This is what autobiography is – a likeness or metaphor of the self. It is an attempt to tell your story in such a way that the self, your essence or 'master form,' as Roy Pascal says, emerges. The reader as well as the writer of a good autobiography should be able to glimpse the self and say, 'Aha! There it is!' When we write an autobiography we move from the known to the unknown; we attempt to grasp the unknown, the mystery of the self, through the known, the myriad details of the story of one's own life. The details are *not* the self, but they ought to point to it, be a metaphor of it. No one's life is complete chaos with no order at all; the details *do* contain a discernible pattern (though maybe not only one, and maybe not a very clear one). To become what I am not, I must start with what I am; but by seeing a pattern emerging in the tapestry I can weave it now more clearly, I can choose to become my emerging self (or

have revealed' (Hannah Arendt, *The Human Condition* [Chicago: University of Chicago Press, 1958], pp. 181–182). Likewise, I would suggest 'who' a Christian is is known only in action–belief and language must be *shown* in action, in life.

* Hans Frei makes very much the same point in regard to 'who' Jesus was, for Jesus was known only in his action, notably in the Passion Story. 'Here he was most of all himself. He *was* this transpiring of circumstances in action. It is equally right to say of his resurrection that here his identity is most fully *manifest*. . . .The two forms [the crucifixion and the resurrection], in their dramatic transition, constitute a unity. In both one may say, "here he was most of all himself" and mean by this expression not a mythological figure but the specific man named Jesus of Nazareth' (Hans Frei, 'Theological Reflections on the Gospel Accounts of Jesus' Death and Resurrection,' *The Christian Scholar*, 49 [Winter 1966], pp. 291–292). Again, we must raise the question of 'who' a Christian is and how we see that our action must be a response to his action, for who we are as Christians is formed by his story.

perhaps radically change – self-knowledge can lead to conversion as well as to emergence).

And the stories of others help also, for what we want from other autobiographies is finally *self-knowledge*. Not only from my own story do I learn who I am, but also from the stories of others. 'What one seeks in reading autobiography is not a date, a name, or a place, but a characteristic way of perceiving, of organizing, and of understanding, an individual way of feeling and expressing that one can somehow be related to oneself.'[9] Thus we have answered the question why we read autobiographies – they help us to reflect on ourselves. This is, I believe, at the heart of the perennial fascination with the story of Jesus (not the theology of his person and work but the story in the synoptic gospels): there is, often even among agnostics, the suspicion that if I knew his story better, I would somehow come to know myself better. Or, as John Dunne says, we 'pass over' to the story of Jesus and to the stories of others and then pass back to ourselves in the quest for self-knowledge.[10] In reading an autobiography, the finger finally points to the reader – and what about *you*? Autobiographers attempt to tell *effective* stories. Martin Buber writes in the Preface to his collection of Hasidic tales about the difference between *telling* and *being* a story.

A rabbi, whose grandfather had been a disciple of the Baal Shem, was asked to tell a story. 'A story,' he said, 'must be told in such a way that it constitutes help in itself.' And he told: 'My grandfather was lame. Once they asked him to tell a story about his teacher. And he related how the holy Baal Shem used to hop and dance while he prayed. My grandfather rose as he spoke, and he was so swept away by his story that he himself began to hop and dance to show how the master had done. From that hour on he was cured of his lameness. That's the way to tell a story!'[11]

Like parables and the parable that is Jesus, religious autobiographies should be effective stories that constitute help in themselves. The finger points as it does in the parabolic form to the reader but in a way that helps to move the reader to begin to integrate his or her own thought and life.

The Art of Autobiography

The reason why an autobiography can be an effective story is that it is not merely a series of personal jottings and reminiscences but a work of art of a peculiar sort. Like a parable, an autobiography tells a particular kind of story, a metaphorical story. That is, the autobiography is intended to be a metaphor of the self; the story has a purpose but that purpose, the revelation of the self, is realized only in and through the details of an actual, historical life. As Roy Pascal says, the main point to an autobiography is the manifestation of 'who' someone is and this occurs only as the reader identifies with the process, the voyage of discovery.

> The truly autobiographical impulse is to recapture the past, to see one's life as a whole, to find within its vagaries one rapture and one indivisible personality. . . .The life is represented in auto-biography not as something established but as a process; it is not simply the narrative of the voyage, but also the voyage itself. . . . This is the decisive achievement of the art of autobiography: to give us events that are symbolic or the personality as an entity unfolding not solely according to its own laws, but also in response to the world it lives in. Through them both the writers and readers know life. It is not necessarily or primarily an intellectual or scientific knowledge, but a knowing through the imagination, a sudden grasp of reality through reliving it in the imagination, an understanding of the feel of life, the feel of living.[12]

The main components of the art of autobiography are all included in this passage: the concern with the self, the importance of a dominant point of view, the harmony between outward events and inward growth, and the similarity between the kind of 'knowing' we call aesthetic and that which comes from the writing and the reading of autobiography. Let us look at each of these in turn very briefly.

The concern with the self. If we understand the term 'self' to be a modern version of 'soul,' which I think it is, then we can see a continuity through confessions and autobiographies ranging all the way from Paul through Augustine up to Sam Keen. There are various degrees of this concern, but throughout it is true to say that genuine autobiographies can be written only by men and women pledged to their innermost selves. It is, of course, this same impulse, this dedication to the innermost self, that lies behind Kierkegaard's *Sickness Unto Death*. One must *appropriate* the self, become what one is; it is a process of creation, of becoming, of drawing being out of nothingness. 'By relating itself to its own self, and by willing to be itself, the self is grounded transparently in the Power which posited it.'[13] It is evident, by the way, that autobiography is a form peculiarly appropriate for the mature: young people may write autobiographical novels, as they often do (Sylvia Plath's *The Bell Jar*, Thomas Wolfe's *Look Homeward, Angel*, James Agee's *A Death in the Family*), but it is somewhat presumptious and inappropriate for a young person to write an autobiography, unless, as in the case of Malcolm X, his or her life is part of a larger struggle and he sees that life drawing to a close, as Malcolm X surely did.

Dominant point of view. Along with a concern with the self, there must be a dominant vision of that self, and this is perhaps the single most important factor in an autobiography.* George Fox's autobiography lacks this quality despite the courageous quality of his actual life; it is composed of sentences and incidents strung together by a series of 'ands' with no dominant unity.[14] Likewise John Stuart Mill fails to create an image of his emotive self; the force or forces that made him what he was, the emotive driving force never takes individual shape. Each incident in a good autobiography should be seen as part of a process, an unfolding; disparate incidents should be bound together from a particular point of view and given thereby 'sense,' 'meaning.' Montaigne called this dominant motif a person's 'master form.'

Harmony between outward events and inward growth. The above comments on point of view or dominant motif move us immediately into the third prerequisite of a good autobiography, the harmony

---

* 'Nearly always some theoretical and intellectual interest in religion, politics, or art plays a leading role in the confession. It is his success in integrating his mind on such subjects that makes the author of a confession feel that his life is worth writing about' (Northrop Frye, *Anatomy of Criticism: Four Essays* [New York: Atheneum, 1968], p. 308).

between outward events and inward growth. Many autobiographies fail because they do not create a significant meeting place between the individual and the outer world; they do not rise to the level of symbolic event in which world and character are embodied. For instance, the confessions of too many medieval mystics take place entirely within their own heads and their own feelings – there is no contact with the outer world; conversely, many hastily written autobiographies by movie personalities and 'interesting' people simply recount events in which they were involved without meshing those events with their own growth. The master form must be seen not merely as an ideal (though it is partly that), but as the *actual* determining factor that in the myriad details of the person's life, his or her action and reaction in particular circumstances, has molded the individual. If an autobiographer has failed to pull that off, we can say that the autobiography is not 'true,' that is, the author has not shown us what really makes him or her tick, though he or she might have told us a number of interesting things. We must be brought to feel that we have *seen the person*, be able to say, 'Yes, here she is, what she claims as the driving force of her life really has been so, in this instance and in that.' Pascal feels that Augustine accomplishes this meshing of the dominant motif (the inner) with the outward circumstances magnificently. If one says that the dominant passion of Augustine is his vision of the grace of God, then this must be *shown* in the actual events of his life, and this Augustine did. It is this integration of the inner and the outer, of the overriding passion and the 'insignificant' details that is the heart of great autobiography, and constitutes what I have called its parabolic quality.

Aesthetic and autobiographical knowing. We have been brought naturally to our final prerequisite for autobiographical writing – autobiography as an art form – by way of the above comments on the patterned or integrated personality revealed through the process of meshing the inner and the outer. For the *process* in an autobiography, the unfolding of the personality, is very similar to the novel form; in fact the autobiographical form, the introspective story of a person searching for and showing his or her master form, greatly influenced the history of the novel. The novel is a late genre, appearing in its modern form only in the eighteenth century, and the psychological complexity of the modern novel owes much to the confessional and autobiographical tradition.[15] There are other similarities as well: both are stories, dependent primarily on *process*, on historical, dramatic movement to reveal personality; in both, human life is understood not as a state of being but as a process of development. A person can be known only in the story of his or her life – discovery is crucial. The novel concerns the innocent in search of an identity, while the autobiography is the backward glance over a life from the point of view of that identity, but the novel and the autobiography have the same tension and meshing of the inner and outer; 'meaning' in both is understood in terms of a pattern incarnated in details and concrete events, both arising from them and interpreting them.* And this, of course, is but another way of saying that the events are parabolic or metaphorical – they have extensions beyond themselves, they are richly complex images embodying the secret of a person's life, as, for instance, the moment in the garden is a metaphor of Augustine's life.

The 'knowing,' then, that takes place both for the writer and the reader of autobiography is not unlike the 'knowing' that takes place in relation to aesthetic objects. I understand aesthetic knowing as wisdom, or getting in on the feel of life; it is not conceptual or scientific knowing but a grasping of the feel of life through the imagination. If this is so, what, then, is the 'truth' or 'value' of such knowing? Roy Pascal says that autobiographical and aesthetic truth is the truth not of knowing but of being, for it has to do primarily not with knowing something but with living life.[16]

Let us approach this question of the truth and value of autobiography in a somewhat oppositional fashion by contrasting biography and autobiography. Many have said that autobiography cannot be trusted because a person looking back over his or her life distorts facts, omits material, remembers incidents erroneously. The biographer is concerned with the 'facts,' with getting things straight, and

---

* 'Autobiography is another form which merges with the novel by a series of insensible gradations. Most autobiographies are inspired by a creative, and therefore fictional, impulse to select only those events and experiences in the writer's life that go to build up an integrated pattern. This pattern may be something larger than himself with which he has come to identify himself, or simply the coherence of his character and attitudes. We may call this very important form of prose fiction the confession form, following St. Augustine, who appears to have invented it, and Rousseau, who established a modern type of it' (Frye, *Anatomy of Criticism*, p. 307).

historians often suspect the perspective of the autobiographer. But of course the crucial difference between the biographer and the autobiographer is that the one presents an external history and the other an internal history.* Both have their rights, and there is no final way to adjudicate between them. Both are 'true,' though in different senses. The one form is close to the photograph, the other to the self-portrait, though that analogy fails to bring in the dynamic process which is the heart of autobiography and the clue to its truth and value. For I would want to say that an autobiography is 'true,' regardless of errors of fact or omissions, if the dominant motif or the self is revealed through interaction with the world by way of dramatic process. The inside view is a true one and hence valuable if the persona, the mask, the plan, the ideal is indeed the consistent ruling theme of the self that emerges and if we have been *shown* that it is. The truth of an autobiography is not the imitation of details or external facts but the consistency of the ordering pattern or master form in relation to the person's encounters with the world. As with a novel, it is not the flashes of insight that count but the total cumulative effect, and this is an achievement of a high aesthetic and interpretive order. Some things count against it, such as over-writing, blurring of the past, embellishment, triviality, and vanity. Its success is a literary as well as a moral accomplishment, for the embellishment and the triviality, when they occur, are a literary as well as a moral failure. In order for the reader to be able to say, 'Yes, here's the person,' the accomplishment must have integrity both as an art object (it must be unified and patterned in an aesthetically satisfying way) and as a moral reality (the imagery must be evocative in such a way that the reader is brought to 'feel' that the

---

* H. Richard Niebuhr's statement on this point is very helpful. 'It is one thing to perceive from a safe distance the occurrences in a stranger's life and quite a different thing to ponder the path of one's own destiny, to deal with the why and whence and whither of one's own existence. Of a man who has been blind and who has come to see, two histories can be written. A scientific case history will describe what happened to his optic nerve or to the crystalline lens, what technique the surgeon used or by what medicines a physician wrought the cure, through what stages of recovery the patient passed. An autobiography, on the other hand, may barely mention these things but it will tell what happened to a self that had lived in darkness and now saw again trees and sunrise, children's faces and the eyes of a friend. Which of these histories can be a parable of revelation, the outer history or the inner one, the story of what happened to the cells of a body or the story of what happened to a self?' (*The Meaning of Revelation* [New York: The Macmillan Co., 1955], pp. 59–60).

autobiographer's interpretation is true; it is, in other words, his or her master form).

This all comes finally to saying that truth in autobiography is never final, for the very process of writing the work changes the author – Montaigne says, 'I have not made my book more than my book has made me' – and the reader of a good autobiography might also say that it has, in some sense, 'made' him or her also.

It is evident that what the reader gets from autobiography is a form of *practical wisdom*. Roy Pascal says of autobiography: 'What it can do is to show how men, at grips with powerful forces within themselves, and in their circumstances, can come to some sort of terms with them.'[17] If art gives, as Susanne Langer says, 'intuitive knowledge of some unique experience,' it is certainly also true of autobiography that it gives knowledge that is quite as true as any other sort as far as the job of living is concerned. Autobiographies give practical wisdom because they are the story of the engagement of a personality in a task, not of the task alone. It is this peculiar meshing of life and thought that is the heart of the matter with autobiographies and which is, I believe, their importance for religious reflection.

Religious Autobiographies

The autobiography altogether is not an appropriate means to urge the objective truth of a doctrine – though it may reveal more profound and general truths of life which the doctrine only partially formulates.[18]

Here we see the connections with both the parabolic form – indirect communication – and the Pauline method of doing theology where there is no separation between theology and life. To say that life and thought are one means that truth equals commitment; it is to say that the master form must be dramatized in the stuff of an individual's existence; it must be lived out. As in Paul's or Augustine's case, one *does theology* and one *theologizes life*. In this perspective, theology becomes a story, a very personal story, as personal as lyric poetry – and as revealing. It is on a continuum with the parable – a dominant decision that binds the inner and outer world, a master form that allows us to say of the Prodigal Son and of Augustine, 'Yes, *here* is the man.' The lines in a parable and in Augustine's *Confessions* are not blurred and fuzzy; each presents, either in capsule form or in an extended metaphor, the overriding passion and decision that make a person what he or she is. Parables are for bringing people to commitment, and while the goal is less direct in autobiographies, the possibility of commitment is still there for the reader. It is a parabolic or Socratic possibility; that is, not 'do as I do,' but 'see what I am' and then enter into your own soul and discover *your* prime direction, your master form, your center and focus. It is existential theology with a vengeance; it is the *living* of belief, not the talking *about* it or the systematizing of it.

The theologian-autobiographer becomes not the vessel of an idea or belief (a spatial metaphor), but a map of the movement of a belief in a human life (a linear metaphor). Autobiographies are paradigms, as parables are; they are contemplative possibilities which can have an indirect effect on others; they give no rules and recite no doctrines but present us with some *possibilities* for living out.

We will look briefly at some confessional statements – those of Paul, Augustine, John Woolman, Sam Keen, and Teilhard de Chardin – to see in what ways they are on a continuum with that basic genre. One of the things we note at the outset is that only one of the above is actually an autobiography – Augustine's *Confessions* (and even it is set within the genre of prayer) – while the rest are mixed genres. Given the propensity of the genre of autobiography to self-absorption, it is important to note the ways in which our authors have avoided too much concern with the self, or, to phrase it otherwise, have understood the self *vocationally*. The letter, the prayer, the journal have served as ways of diverting attention from the self.

Paul. We start with Paul, for his epistles display many of the characteristics of Christian confessions of the mixed genre. Robert Funk makes a crucial point concerning the relation of the parable to Paul's language and to all subsequent Christian language.

If the parable is that mode of language which founds a world, and that particular world under the domain of God's grace, all other language in the Christian tradition is derivative in relation to it. It is out of this 'poetic' medium that the tradition springs, however far in fact it may subsequently wander from it. Paul's language, as well as other languages in the New Testament and early church, presupposes such a foundational language tradition.[19]

Funk goes on to say that discursive theology inevitably moves away from parabolic or foundational language and Paul's case, like all others, must be tested to see 'whether derivative language preserves the intentionality of foundational language.'[20] He believes that Paul's language does indeed pass muster, for it 'intends the world established by the parable.'[21] More precisely, Paul does not consider God and human beings as entities – his is not a theoretical theology – but he throws the hearer back upon the world of the parable where God, person, and world are held in solution.[22] This is, I believe, a crucial statement concerning Paul's way of doing theology. Some have maintained (that is, Bultmann and his followers) that Paul's and the early church's way of presenting the gospel is didactic – an open, message-oriented way – but Funk's position is that Paul's 'theological method' is on a continuum with the hidden, worldly way of the parables.

The literary form Paul uses, the letter, is, in contrast to, say, the essay, sermon, or vision, on a continuum with the parable. The letter is close to oral speech – the dialogue, accusation, defense, and exclamations of Paul's letters challenge the hearer to listen and behold.* The letter, at least Paul's letters, is also an intermediary form between the parable and the confession. Not only does it keep God, person, and the world in solution as does the parable, but it is wrought out of Paul's own experience and utilizes that experience theologically, as does the confession. It is necessary to be as precise as possible on this point, for the centrality of Paul in his letters, most notably his claims to apostolic authority and his plea to the recipients of his letters to 'imitate' him, ought not to be understood as mere self-absorption. Paul is not at any point in the letters writing

---

* 'The letter, consequently, is an appropriate substitute for oral word – it is as near oral speech as possible – yet it provides a certain distance on the proclamation as event. If the parable is a gesture pointing the way into the kingdom of God, the letter is only one step removed: it wonders why the gesture has been missed' (Funk, *Language*, p. 248).

an autobiography à la Petrarch and Rousseau; he is not in love with himself; he does not find himself 'interesting.' His interest in himself is a vocational interest, and the vocational interest in the self is, I believe, one of the central marks of a genuine Christian confession.* Paul's vocational interest in himself means that throughout his letters he tells his story in order to drive home a point – to illustrate what it means to have confidence in the flesh (Phil. 3:4–17), to refrain from eating or drinking if it deters a brother from salvation (I Cor. 10:31–11:1), to boast in weakness (II Cor. 11:22–33), to authenticate his ministry (I Cor. 15:8–10; Gal. 1:11–2:21).

Paul apparently found his own story extremely useful for his vocation, but his way of thinking theologically implies more than just the usefulness of personal experience as illustrative material. He not only uses himself, but he thinks in and through himself: he takes himself as the human metaphor. He thinks, as has been said of the metaphysical poets, with the blood; he is there in the midst of his own thought. It matters terribly to him to work through the problems of law and grace, faith and works, life in the body and the resurrected life, because these were the concrete, existential issues which he had faced in his own life and which those committed to his charge were facing. The law–grace issue was not a theological conundrum to him but a personal crisis; it calls to mind the agony and immediacy with which contemporary Jewish writers such as Elie Wiesel, Richard Rubenstein, and Emil Fackenheim are attempting to work through the issues of the presence of God and the identity of the Jewish people after Auschwitz.

But for Paul, as for Wiesel, Rubenstein, and Fackenheim, the crisis which precipitates such passionate, immediate, and existential theologizing is by no means narrowly personal or self-absorbed. Not only was Paul there in the midst of his thought; his charges – in Rome, Corinth, Galatia, and Philippi – were there too, and it is the centrality of their presence which keeps his theologizing always

---

* As Amos Wilder puts it, Paul was not an individual letter writer but 'an apostle under mandate.' 'Paul, as he himself says, is only a minister of the word and not a rhetorician. Thus even the signed personal letters of Paul also illustrate the new speech-phenomenon whose feature is, if not anonymity, at least a corporate transcendence of the self through the Spirit. This does not mean what we call "personality" or "individuality" are denied in the new faith, but they are found in a new context according to which they are both humbled and exalted' (*Language of the Gospel*, p. 42).

vocationally oriented. One of our outstanding impressions of Paul's letters is of his deep concern for the recipients of his letters. He writes to the wayward, recalcitrant Corinthians almost apologetically: 'I wish you would bear with me in a little foolishness. Do bear with me! I feel a divine jealousy for you, for I betrothed you to Christ to present you as a pure bride to her one husband' (II Cor. 11:1–2).

It seems as if Paul's theological concern derives principally from his vocational drive; that is, he attempts to think as precisely as possible about relations between God and human beings in order to bring his brothers and sisters to a genuine and permanent commitment. The method and the concern parallel the parables very closely because what Paul's theologizing consists of is metaphor after metaphor attempting to evoke indirectly the graciousness of God for the purpose of winning commitment to him. It is difficult to read Paul's theology as metaphorical because his metaphors have become 'stenolanguage,' dead clichés, accepted dogma for us. But his was a fantastically fertile imagination, using anything at hand – tents, bodies, buildings, kernels, homes, flesh. Metaphors spill from him – slaves and sons, flesh and spirit, Adam and Christ, body and members, home and away from home – with the ingenuity of a man who was himself living the thing he was attempting to convey. His metaphors are so good, they work so well, because they are not off the top of his head but are hammered out both through the agony and passion of his own life and through his commitment to the lives of his charges. Many of them came out of a world-view already at hand, of course, but Paul renews them by setting them in the context of God's radical love, the unfamiliar that provides a new context for the familiar so that it is seen anew.

The following passage is typical of Paul's use of metaphor to convey the unconveyable, in this instance, the nature of the future life.

For we know that if the earthly tent we live in is destroyed, we have a building from God, a house not made with hands, eternal in the heavens. Here indeed we groan, and long to put on our heavenly dwelling, so that by putting it on we may not be found naked. For while we are still in this tent, we sigh with anxiety; not that we would be unclothed, but that we would be further clothed, so that what is mortal may be swallowed up by life. He who has prepared us for this very thing is God, who has given us the Spirit as a guarantee. So we are always of good courage; we know that while we are at home in the body we are away from the Lord, for we walk by faith, not by sight. We are of good courage, and we would rather be away from the body and at home with the Lord.

(II Cor. 5:1–8)

It is no coincidence, I believe, that Paul's theology is, in genre as well as in method, parabolic or metaphorical. That is, the genre of his theology, the letter, and his method, metaphorical, go together. The passionate, immediate, existential challenge which he poses in his letters demanded radical theologizing, the creation of new metaphors which would renew the perception and stimulate the commitment of his hearers. A letter is an implied dialogue and it incites the writer to question any staleness and irrelevancy in his address. In his letters Paul has given us a form of theology which in varying ways has been the model for many in the church who have realized that the desperate maneuver of the parabolic way, the hidden way, both in language and in life, may be the only maneuver possible.

Augustine. There are many ways to read the *Confessions*, and so much interpretation and praise have been heaped upon it that one hesitates to do anything other than read the book and wonder at the accomplishment. Roy Pascal notes that it is the first real autobiography and in many ways the greatest. Augustine is the first modern man, the first one to toil in the 'heavy soil' of his own memory in order to recollect his own spiritual evolution, not in terms of a portrait but in terms of a movement in perspective.

It is easy enough to praise the *Confessions* as a great autobiography; it is harder to specify why it is in the tradition of parabolic or metaphorical theology. As all know, Augustine was in some sense or other both a Neoplatonist and a mystic; the *Confessions* is in the form of a prayer to God; the perspective seems self-absorbed rather than vocationally-oriented. But Augustine seems to have something other than his own salvation in mind:

But to whom am I telling this? Not to Thee, O my God, but in Thy presence I am telling it to my own kind, to the race of men or rather to that small part of the human race that may come upon these writings. And to what purpose do I tell it? Simply that I and any other who may read may realise out of what depths we must cry to Thee. For nothing is more surely heard by Thee than a heart that confesses Thee and a life in Thy faith.[23]

This is surely part of what he has in mind – his life as a paradigm for others – but there is another and deeper concern, the unification of his thought with his life, the stages of his own spiritual evolution, not, I believe, simply as a self-authenticating project, but as a vocationally necessary act. That is, knowing and doing, belief and act, had to come together, be *seen* together, in his own life for him to be the kind of theologian he felt called to be.

And this Your word to me would be a lesser thing if it merely commanded me by word and did not go before me in the doing. Thus I do it, in deed and in word, I do it under Your wings and subject to You, and my infirmity known to You.[24]

In the *Confessions* Augustine formulates the crucial dictum of the existentialists – knowing is becoming.[25] Praising God cannot be merely an intellectual thing but must become a living fact in his own life. As David Burrell says, 'As bishop and as theologian, he must speak of God and the things of God. But where does he himself stand? How can he responsibly speak of such things, as distinguished from analytically or defensively?'[26]

The answer lay in the autobiographical form, for only by this means can he speak of God in a way that is not merely off the top of his head. As Burrell notes, if Augustine's crucial theological insight is the assertion that 'to be' is 'to be related to God the Creator,' then he must undertake 'to trace his way to God, the manner in which the relatedness of every creature to the Creator was exhibited in his case. . . .Metaphysical schemes become dramatized when the context is the history of human subjectivity.'[27]

Augustine was an intellectual and a theologian of a high order – a metaphysician like unto few others who have existed; he was concerned with fundamental and highly complex theological assertions throughout the whole of life. So it is even more remarkable that his most metaphysical assertions always backtrack upon *himself*.

Throughout the *Confessions* the pattern of theological assertion and existential appropriation is followed: those assertions about being related to the creator are set in the context of his own relatedness and unrelatedness to the creator. Or, in many instances, the theological assertions arise out of personal reflection, as in the reflections on the boyhood incident of the stolen pears which move naturally into a discussion of all evil as the perversion of good. The fact that the entire work is addressed to God – arguments as well as prayers – means that there are no impersonal assertions about God, only personal witnesses to the meaning of God-talk. As Burrell puts it, 'The rules of inference which govern a particular language must become the rules of one's life if he is to use that language with confidence and alacrity. . . .Language is a way of life, and a confident use of language demands a consonant way of living.'[28]

This is so crucial a point that it is hard to overemphasize it, for it is, I think, at the heart of doing theology rightly. It is the hidden way of parabolic theology, the indirection of incarnation. The thing about using Christian language, in contrast to using Neoplatonic language, as Augustine saw, is directly related to the one thing that Christianity had and Neoplatonism lacked: the embodied word. Neoplatonism had the 'insight,' the awareness that all things are related to God (it even understood that they can be symbolic), but it lacked the word made flesh, the discipline of relating that word to each and every human life and event, including one's own life and events.[29]

When this finally came home to Augustine, he was in a position to become a Christian, and becoming a Christian meant for him undertaking the discipline of making the language he used his way of life. For Augustine, then, the incarnation means something quite definite for the Christian: it means that understanding certain things, things which bear upon his or her own existence, cannot be understood unless he or she is prepared to embody them.[30] The task of becoming a Christian, and particularly of becoming a theologian, one who speaks about God, one who dares to break the silence, is therefore a long process, a dialectic of insight from God and a concomitant struggle on his or her side to incarnate that insight into his or her own life. 'Before we can possess what we have glimpsed, we must undertake a style of life which embodies some of the syntax of the new language adumbrated in the original insight.'[31]

What Augustine does in the *Confessions* is to show us the movement of that process of insight and appropriation, of grace and of
the struggle to incarnate it. He gives us a rare model of a theological
style which I believe is commensurate with the gospel – God with
us – and which ought to serve as a corrective to theological styles
where knowing is not becoming but simply knowing. His is a parabolic theology, the embodiment of Christian language in a way of
life. He does not tell us what to do or how to speak theologically,
but by showing us how God is related to all creatures through the
story of his own experience of coming to belief, he provides us with
a rare model of metaphorical theology.

John Woolman. John Woolman, an eighteenth-century American
Quaker, is solidly within the tradition of great 'parabolic' autobiographers, though his *Journal* is not really an autobiography in the purest
sense, for he avoids heavy concentration on himself.[32] But I have
suggested that interest in the self as 'the medium of the message'
is one of the marks of genuine Christian confession, and Woolman's
Journal meets this criterion with rare excellence. It is astonishing
that this should be the case, for the Puritan spiritual autobiography
was a self-absorbed genre, dedicated to convincing the elders that
grace was manifest in the writer's experience.[33] The medieval-
Petrarchan-Rousseauvian pattern of self-oriented autobiography was
one pattern; the vocationally-oriented autobiography is quite another,
and Woolman's *Journal* is definitely of the latter sort. This second
pattern, I have been maintaining, is the distinctively Christian or
parabolic one, and it is one that obviates self-absorption through
the use of genres such as the journal, the letter, and prayer related
to but less directly concerned with the self than autobiography.

Yet the interesting feature of Christian confession that avoids
concentration on the self is a self-portrait more compelling than the
self-exalting variety. Surely one reason for this apparent contradic-
tion is that the mystery of the self, like all mystery, is visible only
indirectly, through the encounters of the self with the world. It is the
vocationally-oriented autobiographies, those that point away from a
direct, inward perception of the self to what drives the self, drives
it concretely in the world, which are the most revealing of the self.
The writings of Frederick Douglass, Bonhoeffer, and Malcolm X
illustrate the point, while Dag Hammarskjöld's *Markings* gives us

only a vague image of an inner man who might have been 'any' man, so that we must constantly remind ourselves as we read that the writer is the same as the very public Hammarskjöld of the United Nations. There is no 'outer' to define and let us glimpse the 'inner'; it is not parabolic.

But Woolman's *Journal* is a parabolic book both in literary method and content. The overall form of the *Journal* is a recounting of his journeys as an itinerant Quaker missionary: the book itself is a journey, as he saw his life to be. He writes,

> I have gone forward, not as one travelling in a road cast up, and well prepared, but as a man walking through a miry place, in which there are stones here and there, safe to step on; but so situated that one step being taken, time is necessary to see where to step next.[34]

The simile of a journey, a timeful, difficult journey points to Woolman's belief that the perception and articulation of truth is never a direct business. One cannot, he believed, convince others through logic of the validity of a position, convince them, that is, so that they will *live* the position – they must be brought along the same path he himself had gone, so they can see for themselves. Reasons do not convince, for reasons can always be given on both sides. Through painful experiences Woolman had been brought to an astounding clarity of vision concerning the oppressed state of the blacks and the American Indians; his understanding of and sympathy for the poor and downtrodden had resulted in an uncompromising attitude toward the indulgence of the wealthy, indulgence which fanned out into a network of oppression. He refused to wear dyed clothing because the dyes were transported on slave-manned ships from the West Indies, and he refused to use the mails because of the treatment of the slave boys who attended the post horses.

These acts of protest, which in another person might have been merely idiosyncratic gestures, or in our day might be calculated as political protest, were in Woolman directly related to his gradual perception of God's universal love, his love for all people equally. Woolman's theology is painfully simple – God created all, redeemed all, owns all – and from these tenets it is obvious that slavery, excessive wealth, the oppression of any person by another are abso-

lutely unfounded. This is the true situation, as Woolman saw it;
but selfish greed clouds our vision so that in innumerable small
ways we are able to keep ourselves from seeing it clearly. The crude
economic basis of the enslavement of our brothers and sisters must
be made visible, but Woolman knew from talking with slaveholders
and people of great wealth that the direct approach, the approach
by argument, did not work.*

The journey on which the *Journal* takes the reader is the sort
that reflects Woolman's remark, 'Conduct is more convincing than
language.' He maintains a low profile throughout in both conduct
and language, for what he does is to describe in simple but highly
effective prose – the plain style of the Quaker – his own journey to
the truth of the universal love of God. The actual route contains very
few eulogies on God's love; rather it concerns itself with unbiased
descriptions of nights spent in the homes of wealthy slaveholders,
life in the steerage on a trans-Atlantic crossing, meetings in Indian
villages. The route, in other words, is devious. The clear perception
of the Indian's life and the sense of the universal dimensions of his
suffering in the following passage are typical of Woolman's style of
pointing to God's love for all people only in connection with concrete
occurrences.

> Near our tent, on the sides of large trees peeled for that purpose,
> were various representations of men going to and returning from
> the wars, and of some being killed in battle. This was a path
> heretofore used by warriors, and as I walked about viewing those
> Indian histories, which were painted mostly in red or black, and
> thinking on the innumerable afflictions which the proud, fierce

---

* As Daniel Shea remarks on Woolman's method, 'it would be necessary in some
way to bring readers of the *Journal* to the same conclusions he had reached by the
same path he had followed. He had not been argued into the positions he maintained:
he had been brought to see, with absolute clarity of vision in the Light, that the forces
contending for supremacy in the world were divine Love, selfless and expansive, and
self-love, a counterfeit of the other, a disease that lives but gave no life and that
nourished and extended itself by absorbing what there was of life around it. What
Woolman wanted, even more than notional agreement with his arguments, was the
reader's attainment of an equal clarity of vision. He hoped that the purity of Truth,
once clearly seen, would dissolve opposition, and that from the ardor of man's
embrace of Truth would follow compliance with its demands' (Daniel B. Shea, Jr.,
Spiritual Autobiography in Early America [Princeton: Princeton University Press,
1968], p. 64).

spirit produceth in the world, also on the toils and fatigues of warriors in travelling over mountains and deserts; on the miseries and distresses when far from home and wounded by their enemies; of their bruises and great weariness in chasing one another over the rocks and mountains; of the restless, unquiet state of mind of those who live in this spirit, and of the hatred which mutually grows up in the minds of their children, – the desire to cherish the spirit of love and peace among these people arose very fresh in me.[35]

It is impossible to separate the content from the structure of the *Journal*, apart, that is, from rather commonplace paraphrases. Woolman's theology is Paul's and Augustine's – all things belong to God – and like Paul and Augustine, Woolman's impressive achievement is his persistence in carrying this theology through in his life with unrelenting integrity. *That* is the content and structure of the *Journal* and the reason why the *Journal* is parabolic or metaphorical. It is a successful attempt to render the graciousness of God, his love for all people, in the concrete details of an actual life, for the purpose not of encouraging others to follow the author but of helping them to perceive what is so difficult to perceive – the presence of the gracious God in the complex ambiguity of economic and social life.

The degree to which Woolman achieved his vocation, his service to the God of universal love, is indicated in a vision he reports in his *Journal*, a vision in which he imagined he was dead and had forgotten his own name.

Being then desirous to know who I was, I saw a mass of matter of a dull gloomy color between the south and the east, and was informed that this mass was human beings in as great misery as they could be, and live, and that I was mixed with them, and that henceforth I might not consider myself as a distinct or separate being.[36]

He reports that he perceived that the meaning of the angel's words in his vision, 'John Woolman is dead,' meant 'the death of my own will.' Only a Christian confession, not a Petrarchan-Rousseauvian autobiography, could come out at the point of finding the self mixed up with a dull gloomy mass of human beings. But it is the same point at which Paul and Augustine arrived, and Woolman at this juncture in his narrative quotes Gal. 2:20 ('I have been crucified with Christ . . .'). The peculiarity of the Christian confession is the denial of the self, its hiddenness in and for the vocation, the calling to allow the story of the self to be used as an indirect route to insight for others. It eventuates, however, in a vivid self-portrayal, in an individuality that is not that of an 'interesting personality' but of someone molded by God, similar to the great figures of the Old Testament as Erich Auerbach writes of them.

God chose and formed these men to the end of embodying his essence and will – yet choice and formation do not coincide, for the latter proceeds gradually, historically, during the earthly life of him upon whom the choice has fallen. . . .Fraught with their development, sometimes even aged to the verge of dissolution, they show a distinct stamp of individuality entirely foreign to the Homeric heroes. Time can touch the latter only outwardly, and even that change is brought to our observation as little as possible; whereas the stern hand of God is ever upon the Old Testament figures; he has not only made them once and for all and chosen them, but he continues to work upon them, bends them and kneads them, and, without destroying them in essence, produces from them forms which their youth gave no grounds for anticipating.[37]

A Christian writing a confession of God's dealings in his or her life for the purpose of enlightening others indirectly emerges with this sort of individuality, a timeful individuality heavy with the discipline of a heart and will being formed in God's service.

Sam Keen. The choice of Sam Keen is perhaps arbitrary and unfair; after all, we are skipping over Teresa of Avila, Søren Kierkegaard, Frederick Douglass, Leo Tolstoy, and Albert Schweitzer. But Keen's *To a Dancing God* is, to my mind, such an excellent example of a nonparabolic confession that it is irresistible. It is of mixed genre, not an autobiography, but it comes close to the form of autobiography in its intense concentration on the self. In the five meditations or reflections loosely organized around crucial incidents

and experiences in his life, Keen's absorption with the self is everywhere and always evident. His central question appears to be, 'How
may I live gracefully in time?'[38] and this question can be answered, he
believes, by meditating on his own story. 'I have found it necessary to
search for the foundations of my identity and dignity in the intimate,
sensuous, idiosyncratic elements of my own experience. . . .'[39] He
ceases to ask the question What must I do? and concentrates on
Who am I? The search for the answer must be conducted inwardly,
for any story or history outside his, such as the story of Israel or
of the church, is meaningless. The 'prodigal,' as he says, reaches
home not by appropriating an event in the past – the life, death, and
resurrection of Christ – but through 'the realization that gracefulness
requires nothing but the individual's becoming fully incarnate in
his own body and historical situation. Grace is the natural mark of
a fully human life.'[40]

Augustine also concentrated on the self, more centrally and agonizingly than any but a few others ever have, and yet his *Confessions*
is, I believe, parabolic. The difference lies in the purpose of the
focus. Augustine looked at his own life in order to see the presence
of God in it and hence to give existential validity, personal integrity,
to his theology of the radical dependence of all creatures on God.
Keen, living after 'the death of God,' has nothing left but the self,
and a romantic self at that. That is, he does not see the self in terms
of a vocation of any sort – he is not a man with a cause, some notion
of the public good to serve beyond himself – but seeks the self for
its own sake, its own 'gracefulness' and peace. The Christian church
has always had a place for the righteous agnostics, the unconscious
believers, those great humanitarians who have worked in labor
unions, grape fields, native hospitals, and black ghettoes to fight
oppression; who have written, sculpted, and painted in ways which
have helped men and women perceive the dimensions of human
existence; who have invented ways to produce food, control popu-
lations, vaccinate against disease so that human life might be more
liveable. The company of uncanonized saints surely stretches far
into the ranks of the 'unbelievers.' But does it include those for
whom the personal religious question is the primary one – How can
I give *my* life meaning, dignity, purpose?

The direct search for personal satisfaction is, I suspect, a mystical,
elitist, private approach which in its opposition to the public, vulner-

able, concerned way, is contrary to what I have described as parabolic. It is also a false way, in the first instance, because it fails to achieve its goal, a coherent sense of self. At least this is my judgment on the achievement of Keen's book; whether he has achieved something more, apart from the book, is another matter. For the self that comes through the book is one with blurred edges – *who* is he, indeed? He has told us about himself, given dictums about the personal ('If education neglects the intimate, the proximate, the sensuous, the autobiographical, the personal, it fails in its creative task'),[41] laid out a curriculum of courses for heightening the sense of self ('On Becoming a Lover,' 'Introduction to Carnality'), but he himself nowhere emerges as an individual.

I find several reasons for his failure to achieve authentic selfhood. First, Keen's position is intrinsically elitist and therefore basically satisfied.

> Moonlight parties and early love on beaches a continent and a generation away and dreams of a cabin on the evergreen shore of Swan's Island wash together and swirl around with California sand. I am at home in my times: satisfied to be in this place; grateful to have known the wilderness of Tennessee mountains and the ordered calm of Harvard Yard; and – yes – the desert of Palestine which at times flows with milk and honey; pleasantly awaiting the ripening of dreams and the birth of surprises.[42]

As he says elsewhere, his has been a serendipitous life, a life in which nice things happen. The problem of letting the reality or presence of God depend on graceful experiences is that the privileged have most of the nice experiences. Among the once-born, formation of the sort Auerbach talks about in the Old Testament heroes, and which Paul, Augustine, and Woolman exemplify, does not occur. Individuality, after all, is the product not of 'graceful living' but of 'dis-ease.'

Second, and more serious, Keen's search for the self is private, turned inward. Although he makes some cryptic remarks about the relation of attitudes towards one's body to political and social questions ('If . . . my dominant conviction is that my body and my feelings can be trusted, the likelihood is that I will adopt a more liberal view of both political and ultimate reality'[43]) he does not expand these potentially interesting ideas. The public world never seems to impinge on him nor he on it. We never see him in action; what he says he is is never tested in the outer world so that we can see, as Roy Pascal says, the shape that is 'the outcome of the interpenetration and collusion of inner and outer life, of the person and society.'[44] We are not able to say of Keen through reading his book, 'Ah, here's the man!' as we can say of Paul, Augustine, and Woolman, who never focus as directly on the self but use the story of the self to point to something else, the hand of God in human affairs.

Finally, Keen's failure to achieve authentic selfhood seems in large part due to what William Lynch calls a basic lack of trust that the finite, temporal order will get 'anywhere.' Keen, like many today, seems to expect too much, to regard religious certitude on 'the bolt from the blue' pattern, rather than on the venture into the familiar that we have been calling parabolic or metaphorical. Has faith in God in any age ever been anything but a trust in the unseen through its intimations in the concrete and familiar? Has there ever been a direct, open message? Has not the 'message' always been available only by deciphering the hieroglyphics of ordinary, public, historical life? If the parable of Jesus is our guide, we must take very seriously the familiar, ordinary world, working hard with it to discover those dislocations within the familiar which suggest intimations of the gracious unfamiliar. And Keen's way is decidedly not the way of the parable.

Pierre Teilhard de Chardin. My comments on Teilhard will be brief, not because his letters and occasional autobiographical essays do not merit extensive treatment, but because the point I wish to make in relation to him is a limited one. The point: a mystic can be para-bolic.[45] My criticisms of Sam Keen may have suggested that intense concern with the self and its relation 'to what is experienced as holy and sacred' (Keen) is anti-Christian or at least nonparabolic. But that is by no means always the case, as Paul, Augustine, and Wool-man amply illustrate. Teilhard illustrates it also – contempor-aneously, scientifically, magnificently, and eloquently.

No one, I think, will understand the great mystics – St. Francis, and Blessed Angela, and the others – unless he understands the full depth of the truth that *Jesus must be loved as a world.*

Then is it really true, Lord? By helping on the spread of science and freedom, I can increase the density of the divine atmosphere, in itself as well as for me: that atmosphere in which it is always my one desire to be immersed. By laying hold of the Earth I enable myself to cling closely to you. What joy then possesses my mind, with what joy my heart expands![46]

An intense love for the world and an intense love of God united in one's worldly vocation, whatever that might be, is Teilhard's mystical vision and he never tires of saying it over and over in different ways: 'Great love of God normally presupposes the maintenance of a strong natural passion.'[47] 'I feel that the more I devote myself in some way to the interests of the earth in its highest form, the more I belong to God.'[48] 'I want these pages to be instinct with my love of matter and life, and to reconcile it, if possible, with the unique adoration of the only absolute and definitive Godhead.'[49]

The basic parabolic impulse, the perception of the extraordinary in the ordinary, is at dead center of Teilhard's mysticism: '*beneath the ordinariness of our most familiar experiences*, we realize, with a religious horror, that what *is emerging in us is the great cosmos.*'[50] This magnificent vision is no steady state of being but a process, a becoming, a physical and spiritual evolution in which all must participate to bring it about. Teilhard's concern with himself is a vocational concern: the world must be loved more than the self if the vision of the evolution of the world into God is to become a reality. The imagery Teilhard uses constantly is that of struggle, journeying, climbing, building.

If he is to act in conformity with his new ideal, the man who has determined to admit love of the world and its cares into his interior life finds that he has to accept *a supreme renunciation*. He has sworn to seek for himself, in other words to love the world better than himself. He will now have to realize what this noble ambition will cost him. In the first place he must, in any case, work to drive things, and his own being, up the steep slope of liberation and purification, he must discipline or conquer the hostile forces of matter, of the forest and of the heart – he must bring about the victory of duty over attraction, of the spiritual over the sense, of good over evil. . . . The multitude of the dead cry out to him not to weaken, and from the depths of the future those who are waiting for their turn to be born stretch out their arms to him and beg him to build for them a loftier nest, warmer and brighter.[51]

The individual self, Teilhard's sense of his own person, is a microcosm of that struggle to help the great cosmos emerge from the ordinary: 'what fascinates me in life is being able to collaborate in a task, a reality, more durable than myself.'[52] That task as he sees it is nothing less than making himself and the world more and more 'transparent to the Will of God with which nature is charged and impregnated through and through.'[53] Teilhard's is a rare form of the parabolic – the 'familiar' is nothing less than the cosmos itself. The mystical ecstasy is held, however, at all times in the tight grip of the lowly and the hidden, for the penetration of the familiar by God is understood in terms of the heavy historicity of biological evolution and, at the peak of evolution, in terms of the human being's conscious, disciplined, individual cooperation toward completing the evolution of the world into God. As high and as far as Teilhard's hope reaches, it is rooted in his sense for the earth, and its first and already complete expression, in the writings from the trenches, takes the form of a personal and highly imaginative vision seeking fuller conceptualization.

Conclusion

What would theology be like were it to turn to religious autobiography as one of its sources? A certain kind of theology is suggested by the confessions we have looked at, a theology which runs as it writes, tests its tenets in life, finds its materials in the story of life in the world. It would not be afraid to be personal, though it would search for the self and its master form in order to create from it a metaphor or parable of God's way of working in the world. It would realize, with Hannah Arendt, that 'who' the Christian is can never finally be conveyed in generalizations, but only in this and that particular human story. Thus it would realize that belief and language must be dramatized concretely in order for the 'who' to emerge. Moreover, it would insist that who a Christian is is never only a question of the self in isolation, for, first of all, the story of each and every Christian is formed by the story of another, Jesus of Nazareth. The story of each and every Christian is always in the service of that prior story – a Christian autobiography is always vocational. There is another sense in which who a Christian is is never only a private discovery, for that discovery takes place not only through encounter with the story of Jesus but also through encounter with the stories of many others. Language and belief are hammered out in action; they arise from and must return to the social and political worlds in which we find ourselves.* This is true of the search for all real identity, but it is particularly true of Christian identity which is formed in response to the story of one whose life was a parable of God's love for *all* men and women. There can be no such thing as a private Christian autobiography; Christian autobiographies are ineradicably public and that means social and political, as the autobiographies of Paul, Augustine, Woolman, and Teilhard amply testify.

Such parabolic or intermediary theology would realize that theological reflection is always embodied thinking, thought which cannot finally abstract from the person who is doing the thinking. The question always doubles back on the self, for in this kind of reflection there is no way to bracket the self. A Paul or an Augustine understand their lives in some sense as metaphors of their theology and their theology as metaphors of their lives. Life and thought mutually illuminate each other: I come to understand what I believe and the language I use only as I live it, and I am able to live my belief and the language I use only as I come to understand them more clearly. Who am I? The answer is a story, an intricate tale of action and insight, details and emerging order; a tale for the Christian not just of the self, but of the self in the hands of the living God. The pattern that forms in the tapestry – the 'me' that emerges – is not solely of my own doing; it is from, in, and toward God. That is the mystery that the autobiographical theologian deals with. We see into

* Hannah Arendt says that the revelatory quality of speech and action comes about in 'sheer human togetherness.' Neither the doer of good deeds who must remain anonymous nor the criminal who must hide from others can reveal their identity. 'Because of its inherent tendency to disclose the agent together with the act, action needs for its full appearance the shining brightness we once called glory, and which is possible only in the public realm' (*The Human Condition*, p. 180).

such a glass darkly and know little of ourselves, but some day we shall know who we are even as we are now known.

Finally, then, the question doubles back not only on the writer of a religious autobiography, but on the reader as well. As in a parable, so with a religious autobiography, the question is always, 'And who are you?' How is your language and belief integrated with your style of life, your action in the real world? A theology that takes its bearings from religious autobiographies ought always to pose this question, for it is *the* hermeneutical question. It is the primary task of theology to serve the hearing and acceptance of the word of God and it is precisely the implied question of all good religious autobiographies. In many ways, then, religious autobiographies are a parabolic form, for in their personal and existential thrust oriented to the integration of language, belief, and life in the real world of social and political action they are metaphors, new contexts which deform the old story of God's graciousness to us and help us to come to the point where we might say 'Yes' to that extraordinary graciousness.*

We have been looking at the poem, the novel, and the autobiography as parabolic genres – genres which unite the ordinary and the extraordinary, the unsurprising and the surprising, not openly or miraculously but in and through the everyday and the common. I have suggested further that these genres are key resources for a kind of theological reflection which has been a strong undercurrent in the history of Western theology, a history, however, that has been dominated by a more abstract, systematic genre.

Intermediary theology, however, is not *one* kind of theology; that is, there is no one style to which it must conform. To be sure, as a second-order level of reflection upon the parabolic forms of the poem, novel, and autobiography, various attempts at it will have imagistic, narrative, and existential notes, but these attempts will manifest the notes in a variety of ways and emphases. It is, then,

---

* It is obvious, given our stress on the *form* that good or true autobiography should take, that many non-Christian autobiographies can be sources for theological reflection. Autobiographies such as that of Malcolm X, or autobiographical novels such as Elie Wiesel's *Night*, display many of the characteristics we have noted in good Christian autobiographies. The 'vocation' may be different, but the form is in many instances the same, if only because, as many have pointed out, the autobiography is a Western Christian genre, begun by Augustine and forever bearing his mark.

impossible to say precisely *what* parabolic theology is or will be. A few things can be said, however, in addition to the scenarios set forth in my attempts to spell out the general relations between poem, novel, autobiography, and theology.

First, if theologians accorded the same long-term and sophisticated study to the primary literary genres of the Christian tradition as they have to philosophical concepts, we might hope for a level of excellence with regard to this kind of reflection comparable to the level of excellence in systematic theology. Too often the only kind of theology available to the layperson is journalistic and second-rate. There is little between primary religious reflection (the parable and its accompanying genres) and academic theology that is first-rate reflection. A handful of names come to mind, perhaps, but it simply is the case that theologians have not, for the most part, attended to the parabolic resources with the same rigor, passion, and commitment that they have attended to the resources from philosophy. The first thing to be said, then, is that these resources demand such attention, and were it given, first-rate reflection, of varying styles and emphases, could and ought to result.

The last comment leads to a second point. Parabolic or intermediary theology will, of necessity, be of many sorts. This is so for two reasons. First, its task is hermeneutical, and this means that what it attempts is not just a translation or formulation in contemporary terms of old symbols and images but a deformation, a recontextualization, of the tradition. It aims for metaphorical transformation so that the old can be heard and seen anew and hence accepted. The goal is the 'Yes' to the word of God. Something new must always be one partner in a metaphor and it is this necessity for new contexts which militates against *one* style of intermediary theology. Secondly, in parabolic theology the figurer is always ingredient in the figure; that is, parabolic theology is always autobiographical and finally individual. Unlike Kierkegaard's 'professor' who could systematize existence but himself never exist as an individual in passion and inwardness, the intermediary theologian has no such escape. Such theology will always carry, as Hopkins says, 'the taste of me.' Hence such theology is necessarily openended; systematic thought may be closed and finished, but reflection in which one's life is figured into the thought must remain open, hesitant, and unfinished.

The younger Richard Niebuhr is a parabolic or intermediary

theologian when he writes of the ordinary experiences of fear and gladness as basic material for theology:

> We do not as a rule look to such everyday experiences as manifestations having an import for human destiny. And yet in disdaining to place a theological or a religious interpretation upon the ordinary we commit an error. For it is just in this doubleness of experience that we meet and can trace, if you will, the geneses of some of the most influential beliefs of the church – and what is of more importance – can also win a greater understanding of the life in faithful experience that may appropriately call itself Christian.[54]

He goes on to say that Luther's doctrine of justification by grace through faith, for example, is 'not an esoteric piece of Christian gnosis' but is grounded in experiences of both powerlessness and surprising joy and freedom in Luther's own life.

In a similar vein, William Lynch is a parabolic theologian when he says in a recent book that faith is the ability to see the relationship between the promise and the seemingly contrary form in which the promise is realized.

> . . . faith no more than Sophocles treats us as children; it demands active imagining; it is always asking us to put the expected (of the promises of God) together with the historical forms of the unexpected.[55]

Thus Abraham who had been told his 'descendants shall be as the sands of the sea' had to 'educate' his faith to the point where he could put that promise alongside the command to slay Isaac, his only son. 'For faith knows that the promises will be kept, but in what form it does not know.'[56] This is metaphorical thinking of a radical sort, moving from the old to the new, perceiving the old promises in new contexts. As Lynch says so perceptively, 'the true dreamer, or the recomposer of reality, is one who dares to forge a new hypothesis and slowly match it to possibility.'[57] Such is the substance of the capacity to believe in parabolic terms.

'Being religious' or 'reflecting theologically' in the parabolic mode means reading the ordinary events of one's life and times as a parable, that is, seeing those events within a surprising and new context, the context provided by the gracious God. It means starting with where one is and what one has at hand to move beyond that place. The possibility of such movement is implied in the death of Hopkins' nun, the awareness that that graciousness *does* lie ahead, not in the unknown, 'religious' sphere, but as the culmination of all the intimations of grace – that is, the joy and hope and gifts – already known throughout the commonness of individual and social life. 'The profession that God governs the course of human affairs for good is a judgment,' says Richard Niebuhr, 'which puts together the hazards and fortuitous moments of life in the street, life constantly intensified and stretched out in surprising and dismaying events, and affirms that this whole experience – incomplete, asymmetrical, and often dissonant – is good.'[58] Being religious or reflecting theologically in the parabolic mode does not mean being 'a giant of the faith' or having 'religious experiences.' A different orientation to life is assumed by those who take their cues from parables rather than from dogmas or pious sayings. They realize that being secular and skeptical not only is all right, it is necessary; that life is risky and openended; and that surprising things happen *in it*.

To start with the ordinary and the everyday, with personal life, with corporate stories, with 'our times' in their political and social agony, is the bold business of theology. But it is exactly where Jesus' parables start. Daniel Berrigan insists that few if any will be able to understand Jesus' parables until they become skilled at reading the text of the events of their own lives – and ordering their lives accordingly;[59] Augustine knew he would not fully understand the language of Christian faith until he could read it in the familiar events of his own life – and attempt to embody it there anew. Life and thought – personal and social existence *and* 'being religious' or 'thinking theologically' – are so intricately related, so symbiotic, that, difficult as it is, and prone to ambiguity and sentimentality as it can become, there is no escape from the task of thinking with the blood, of being, humbling as it is, 'a body that thinks,' the human metaphor. A theology that takes its cues from the parables has no other course than to accept what may appear to be severe limitations – limitations imposed by never leaving behind the ordinary, the physical, and the historical. But these limitations are the glory of parabolic, metaphoric movement, for they declare that human life in all its complex everydayness will not be discarded but that it is precisely the familiar world we love and despair of saving that is on the way to being redeemed. The central Christian affirmation, the belief that somehow or other God was in and with Jesus of Nazareth, is the ground of our hope that the ordinary is the way to the extraordinary, the unsurprising is the surprising place.

A theology that takes its cues from the parables never reaches its object, but in language, belief, and life as metaphor, story, and living engagement we are sent off in its direction. It is a theology for skeptics and for our time. We make the leap not with our minds alone but with our total selves – our words, our stories, and our life engagement – and wager that we are on the way, that the metaphor sees in a glass darkly what we do not see and cannot know.

Notes

Chapter 1

1. Richard L. Rubenstein, *After Auschwitz: Radical Theology and Contemporary Judaism* (New York: Bobbs-Merrill Co., 1966), p. x.
2. Sam Keen, *To a Dancing God* (New York: Harper and Row, 1970), p. 99.
3. Günther Bornkamm, *Jesus of Nazareth*, trans. Irene and Fraser McLuskey with James M. Robinson (London: Hodder and Stoughton, 1960), pp. 126–127.
4. Dan Otto Via, Jr., *The Parables: Their Literary and Existential Dimension* (Philadelphia: Fortress Press, 1967), p. 172.
5. Ibid., p. 83.
6. Philip Wheelwright, *The Burning Fountain: A Study in the Language of Symbolism* (Bloomington: Indiana University Press, 1968), p. 86.
7. *Poems and Prose of Gerard Manley Hopkins* (London: Penguin Books, 1953), p. 27.
8. Ibid., p. 219.
9. Keen, *To a Dancing God*, pp. 100–101.
10. Ibid., p. 99.
11. Ibid., p 101.
12. Ibid.
13. Ibid., p. 103.
14. Robert W. Funk, 'The Parables: A Fragmentary Agenda,' in *Jesus and Man's Hope*, II, ed. Donald G. Miller and Dikran Y. Hadidian (Pittsburgh: Pittsburgh Theological Seminary, 1971), p. 300.
15. Robert W. Funk, 'Myth and The Literal Non-Literal,' in *Parable, Myth and Language*, ed. Tony Stoneburner (Cambridge, Mass.: The Church Society for College Work, 1968), p. 63.

Chapter 2

1. Amos N. Wilder, *The Language of the Gospel: Early Christian Rhetoric* (New York: Harper and Row, 1964), pp. 13–14.
2. George Steiner, *Language and Silence: Essays on Language, Literature and the Inhuman* (New York: Atheneum, 1972), p. 36.
3. Dallas High, *Language, Persons and Belief: Studies in Wittgenstein's Philosophical Investigations and Religious Uses of Language* (New York: Oxford University Press, 1967), p. 27.
4. Augustine, *The Confessions*, trans. F. J. Sheed (New York: Sheed and Ward, 1942), Bk. 10.6.
5. Edwyn Bevan, *Symbolism and Belief* (New York: Macmillan, 1938), p. 12.
6. Frederick Ferré, 'Metaphors, Models, and Religion,' *Soundings*, 51 (1968), 344.
7. John Dillenberger, 'On Broadening the New Hermeneutic,' *The New Hermeneutic*, ed. James M. Robinson and John B. Cobb, Jr. (New York: Harper and Row, 1964), p. 162.
8. Funk, 'Myth and The Literal Non-Literal,' p. 62.
9. Erich Auerbach, *Mimesis: The Representation of Reality in Western Literature*, trans. Willard Trask (New York: Doubleday and Co., 1957), Chs. 1 and 2.
10. Wilder, *Language of the Gospel*, pp. 64, 65.
11. Owen Barfield, *Speaker's Meaning* (Middletown, Conn.: Wesleyan University Press, 1967).
12. Wilder, *Language of the Gospel*, p. 128.
13. *Poems and Prose of Hopkins*, pp. 30–31.
14. Paul Ricoeur, *The Symbolism of Evil*, trans. Emerson Buchanan (Boston: Beacon Press, 1969).

Chapter 3

1. I. A. Richards, *The Philosophy of Rhetoric* as quoted in Max Black, *Models and Metaphors: Studies in Language and Philosophy* (Ithaca: Cornell University Press, 1962), p. 41.
2. Black, *Models and Metaphors*, p. 41.
3. Ian Ramsey, *Models and Mystery* (London: Oxford University Press, 1964), pp. 13–16.

4. Stanley Burnshaw, *The Seamless Web* (New York: George Braziller, 1970), p. 98.

5. Samuel Coleridge, 'Biographia Literaria,' Ch. 14, *The Portable Coleridge*, ed. I. A. Richards (New York: The Viking Press, 1967), p. 516.

6. Ernst Cassirer, *Language and Myth*, trans. Susanne K. Langer (New York: Harpers, 1946), p. 84.

7. Owen Barfield, *Poetic Diction: A Study in Meaning* (London: Faber and Faber, 1928), p. 141.

8. John Middleton Murry, *Countries of the Mind: Essays in Literary Criticism*, 2nd series (Oxford: Oxford University Press, 1931), p. 1.

9. C. Day-Lewis, *The Poetic Image* (London: Jonathan Cape, 1947), p. 35.

10. Elizabeth Sewell, *The Human Metaphor* (Notre Dame: University of Notre Dame Press, 1964), pp. 11, 200.

11. *Poems and Prose of Hopkins*, p. 5.

12. Barfield, *Speaker's Meaning*, p. 53.

13. Ibid., p. 59.

14. Barfield, *Poetic Diction*, pp. 140–141.

15. Ricoeur, *Symbolism of Evil*, p. 356.

16. Sewell, *Metaphor*, p. 11.

17. Benjamin Ladner, 'On Hearing the Orphic Voice,' *Soundings*, 55 (Summer 1972), 247, 248.

18. Ibid., pp. 240–241.

19. Walter J. Ong, S. J., 'Evolution, Myth, and Poetic Vision,' *New Theology* #5, ed. Martin Marty and Dean Peerman (New York: Macmillan, 1968), pp. 246, 247.

20. Sewell, *Metaphor*, p. 78.

Chapter 4

1. Heinz Politzer, *Franz Kafka: Parable and Paradox* (Ithaca: Cornell University Press, 1962), p. 1.

2. Robert W. Funk, *Language, Hermeneutic and Word of God: The Problem of Language in the New Testament and Contemporary Theology* (New York: Harper and Row, 1966), pp. 193–196.

3. Philip Wheelwright, *Metaphor and Reality* (Bloomington: Indiana University Press, 1962), p. 71.

4. Funk, *Language*, p. 130.

5. Leander Keck, *A Future for the Historical Jesus: The Place of Jesus*

in Preaching and Theology (Nashville: Abingdon Press, 1971), p. 246.

6. C. H. Dodd, *The Parables of the Kingdom* (New York: Scribners, 1961), p. 16.

7. Wilder, *Language of the Gospel*, p. 80.

8. Norman Perrin, 'Historical Criticism, Literary Criticism, and Hermeneutics: The Interpretation of the Parables of Jesus and the Gospel of Mark Today,' *Journal of Religion*, 52 (1972), 361–375.

9. Ibid., p. 365.

10. Ibid., pp. 370–371.

11. Walter J. Ong, 'Voice as Summons for Belief: Literature, Faith, and the Divided Self,' *Literature and Religion*, ed. Giles B. Gunn (New York: Harper and Row, 1971), pp. 68–86.

12. Funk, *Language*, p. 197.

13. Ibid., p. 154.

14. Ibid., pp. 155–156.

15. Perrin, 'Historical Criticism . . . ,' p. 374.

16. Funk, 'The Parables: A Fragmentary Agenda,' p. 295.

17. Ibid., p. 299.

18. Paul Ricoeur, 'Philosophy and Religious Language,' *Journal of Religion*, 54 (January 1974), 76, 78.

19. Keck, *Historical Jesus*, pp. 245, 246.

20. Richard R. Niebuhr, *Experiential Religion* (New York: Harper and Row, 1972), p. 77.

Chapter 5

1. William A. Beardslee, *Literary Criticism of the New Testament* (Philadelphia: Fortress Press, 1970), p. 11.

2. Wilder, *Language of Gospel*, p. 98.

3. Wheelwright, *Metaphor*, p. 51.

4. *English Poetry of the XVII Century*, ed. Roberta Florence Brinkley (New York: W. W. Norton and Co., 1942), pp. 70–71.

5. Ibid., pp. 273–275.

6. *Poems and Prose of Hopkins*, p. 30.

7. T. S. Eliot, *Selected Essays 1917–1932* (New York: Harcourt, Brace, 1932), p. 247.

8. 'Hymns for Now,' *Workers Quarterly*, 39 (July 1967).

9. Wheelwright, *Metaphor*, pp. 72–91.

10. Day-Lewis, *The Poetic Image*, p. 35.

11. Ricoeur, *Evil*, p. 356.
12. Wheelwright, *Metaphor*, pp. 78, 80.
13. Corita Kent, *Footnotes and Headlines: A Book of Play-Prayers* (New York: Herder and Herder, 1967).
14. Good Friday, 'Hymns for Now,' p. 12.
15. The Tree Springs to Life, ibid., p. 13.
16. Andrew Lloyd Webber and Tim Rice, *Jesus Christ Superstar* (Decca Records).
17. Kent, *Footnotes*, p. 16.
18. Ibid., p. 24.
19. Ibid., p. 18.
20. Paul Van Buren, *Theological Explorations* (New York: Macmillan, 1968), p. 170.
21. Paul A. Lacey, *The Inner War: Forms and Themes in Recent American Poetry* (Philadelphia: Fortress Press, 1972), p. 114.
22. Ibid.
23. Denise Levertov, 'Illustrious Ancestors,' from *Overland to the Islands* (1958), quoted in *Anglican Theological Review*, 50 (July 1968), 259.

Chapter 6

1. Wilder, *Language of the Gospel*, pp. 67, 64–65.
2. Ibid., pp. 76–77.
3. Auerbach, *Mimesis*, p. 327.
4. Wilder, *Language of the Gospel*, p. 67.
5. Erich Auerbach, *Dante: Poet of the Secular World*, trans. Ralph Manheim (Chicago: University of Chicago Press, 1961), pp. 174–175, 94–95.
6. William F. Lynch, S. J., *Christ and Apollo: The Dimensions of the Literary Imagination* (New York: New American Library, 1963), p. xiv.
7. Ibid.
8. Ibid., p. 23.
9. Ibid., p. 33.
10. Fyodor Dostoevsky, *The Brothers Karamazov*, trans. Constance Garnett (New York: Random House, 1950).
11. Alan Paton, *Cry, the Beloved Country* (New York: Charles Scribners' Sons, 1950).
12. C. S. Lewis, *Out of the Silent Planet* (New York: The Macmillan Co., 1967).

13. Ibid., p. 42.
14. Charles Williams, *The Place of the Lion* (London: Victor Gollancz Ltd., 1947).
15. Ibid., pp. 45–46.
16. 'Fathers and Heretics,' review of *Fathers and Heretics: Studies in Dogmatic Faith* by G. L. Prestige, *Time and Tide*, November 16, 1940, p. 1123.
17. J. R. R. Tolkien, *The Lord of the Rings*, 3 parts (New York: Ballantine Books, 1970).
18. R. J. Reilly, *Romantic Religion: A Study of Barfield, Lewis, Williams, and Tolkien* (Athens: University of Georgia, 1971), pp. 205, 206.
19. Flannery O'Connor, *The Violent Bear It Away* (New York: Farrar, Straus, and Giroux, 1960).
20. Flannery O'Connor, *Mystery and Manners: Occasional Prose*, ed. Sally and Robert Fitzgerald (New York: Farrar, Straus, and Giroux, 1969), p. 32.
21. Ibid., p. 124.
22. Ibid., p. 42.
23. Stephen Crites, 'Myth, Story, History,' p. 68.
24. William A. Beardslee, *Literary Criticism*, p. 17.
25. Ibid., pp. 16–18.
26. Richard R. Niebuhr, *Experiential Religion*, p. 69.
27. H. Richard Niebuhr, *The Responsible Self: An Essay in Moral Philosophy* (New York: Harper and Row, 1963), pp. 175, 177–178.

Chapter 7

1. Gordon W. Allport, *The Use of Personal Documents in Psychological Science* (New York: Social Science Research Council, 1942), p. 78.
2. Donald Capps and Walter Capps, eds., *The Religious Personality* (Belmont: Wadsworth Publishing Co., 1970), pp. 1–2.
3. Theodore Roszak, *The Making of a Counter Culture: Reflections on the Technocratic Society and Its Youthful Opposition* (New York: Doubleday and Co., 1969), p. 57.
4. James Olney, *Metaphors of Self: The Meaning of Autobiography* (Princeton: Princeton University Press, 1972), p. 23.
5. Ibid., p. 5.
6. Ibid., p. 49.

7. Hannah Arendt, *The Human Condition* (Chicago: University of Chicago Press, 1958), pp. 181–182.

8. Ibid., pp. 187–188.

9. Olney, *Metaphors of Self*, p. 37.

10. John S. Dunne, *A Search for God in Time and Memory: An Exploration Traced in the Lives of Individuals from Augustine to Sartre and Camus* (London: Macmillan, 1969), p. 7.

11. As quoted in Richard A. Underwood, 'Ecological and Psychedelic Approaches to Theology,' *Soundings*, 52 (Winter 1969), 367.

12. Roy Pascal, *Design and Truth in Autobiography* (Cambridge: Harvard University Press, 1960), pp. 24, 182, 185. I am indebted to this excellent book for much of the following material on the nature of autobiography.

13. Søren Kierkegaard, *The Sickness Unto Death*, trans. Walter Lowrie (Princeton: Princeton University Press, 1941), p. 19.

14. John N. Morris, *Versions of the Self: Studies in English Autobiography from John Bunyan to John Stuart Mill* (New York: Basic Books, Inc., 1966), pp,. 117, 118.

15. Pascal, *Autobiography*, pp. 52–53, 187–188.

16. Ibid., p. 98.

17. Ibid., p. 178.

18. Ibid., p. 182.

19. Funk, *Language*, p. 244.

20. Ibid., p. 245.

21. Ibid.

22. Ibid., p. 239–240.

23. Augustine, *Confessions*, Bk. 2.3.

24. Ibid., Bk. 10.4.

25. I am indebted to David Burrell's excellent article, 'Reading The Confessions of Augustine: An Exercise in Theological Understanding,' *Journal of Religion*, 50 (October 1970), 327–351, for the analysis which follows.

26. Ibid., p. 331.

27. Ibid., p. 332.

28. Ibid., p. 339.

29. Augustine, *Confessions*, Bk. 7.9.

30. Burrell, op. cit., p. 337.

31. Ibid.

32. *The Journal of John Woolman* (New York: Corinth Books, 1961).

33. Daniel B. Shea, Jr., *Spiritual Autobiography in Early America* (Princeton: Princeton University Press, 1968), p. 91.

34. 'Concerning the Ministry,' quoted, by Shea, ibid., p. 73.

35. Woolman, *Journal*, pp. 140–141.

36. Ibid., p. 214.

37. Auerbach, *Mimesis*, pp. 14, 15.

38. Keen, *To a Dancing God*, p. 6.

39. Ibid., p. 2.

40. Ibid., p. 23.

41. Ibid., p. 41.

42. Ibid., p. 36–37.

43. Ibid., p. 155.

44. Pascal, *Autobiography*, p. 185.

45. Pierre Teilhard de Chardin, *Writings in Time of War*, trans. Réne Hague (New York: Harpers, 1965); *The Making of a Mind: Letters from a Soldier-Priest 1914–1919*, trans. Réne Hague (London: Collins, 1965).

46. Teilhard, *War*, pp. 148, 138.

47. Ibid., p. 83.

48. Ibid., p. 57.

49. Ibid., p. 14.

50. Ibid., p. 27.

51. Ibid., p. 66.

52. Teilhard, *Letters*, p. 144.

53. Teilhard, *War*, p. 62.

54. Niebuhr, *Experiential Religion*, pp. 104–105.

55. Lynch, *Images of Faith*, p. 22.

56. Ibid., p. 155.

57. Ibid., pp. 119–120.

58. Niebuhr, *Experiential Religion*, p. 71.

59. Daniel Berrigan, *The Dark Night of Resistance* (New York: Doubleday and Co., 1971), p. 70.

Index